Things 90s Kids Realize

Christopher Hudspeth

ISBN-10:1468192426
ISBN-13: 978-1468192421

TABLE OF CONTENTS

INTRODUCTION

Welcome. Before going any further, it is strongly suggested that you read and fully comprehend the **Ten Commandments of 90s Kids.**

I

Thou shalt have no Power Rangers, other than the Mighty Morphin' ones. That means that if they ain't named Zack, Kimberly, Billy, Trini, Jason or Tommy, you shouldn't have anything to do with them. No Power Rangers Time Force, Wild Force, Ninja Storm, Dino Thunder, Mystic Force, Jungle Fury, Samurai, etc. It's Mighty Morphin' or bust.

II

Thou shalt not go chasing water falls. Please stick to the rivers and the lakes that you're used to. If TLC suggested it back in '95, then it's probably still good advice.

III

Thou shalt not take the name of their beloved Skeeter Valentine in vain. Over the years, variations of Doug's best friend's name have been established to mean something rather inappropriate (e.g. "Aw, skeet, skeet!" – Lil Jon). Don't contribute to the popularity of such abysmal vernacular.

IV

Remember Gym Class Parachute Day. A glorious school day that consisted of playing various games with a giant red, green, blue and yellow apparatus. Surely it is a time worthy of weekly remembrance.

V

Honour thy DVD player, iPod and Wi-Fi. Because they used to be VCRs, boom boxes and dial-up internet.

VI

Thou shalt not eat the pizza health on Turtles In Time, if thou already haveth full strength. The person playing with you may need it, don't be a douche. Seriously, plenty of friendships have ended over this.

VII

Girl shalt meet boy and boy shalt meet world. Meaning, if you want to have a perfect relationship, base it 100% off of Cory and Topanga. (Especially season six, they were sooo in love that year.)

VIII

Thou shalt not get in one little fight. Your mom will get scared and make you move in with your Auntie and Uncle in Bel-Air.

IX

Thou shalt be as good of a neighbor as Wilson was to the Taylor family. Remember him from *Home Improvement*? He was a magnificent neighbor and you should be too.

X

Thou shalt not kill their sibling(s) in pursuit of a improving their hierarchy spot/title (e.g. KING). Because *The Lion King* gave some folks the wrong idea.

1. MIGHTY MORPHIN' POWER RANGERS IS NOW A COMEDY.

There was a point in every 90s kid's life where their biggest worry wasn't school, a job or bills – it was whether or not the Power Rangers could survive Rita Repulsa and Lord Zedd's shenanigans. Now, if you re-watch *Mighty Morphin' Power Rangers* today, you'll be amused by the ridiculousness that takes place in *every* single episode. The insults, special effects and characters in general were a mixture of corny & cheesy, which may sound like a delicious concoction -- but is actually impossible to digest without laughing.

Watching the show now has its benefits though; you can appreciate things that you didn't necessarily enjoy in your youth. The hotness of Amy Jo Johnson (Kimberly, the Pink Ranger) is one thing many of us noticed in the 90s, but *really* value as an adult. Johnson's gymnastic skills, all pink clothing/accessories and obnoxiously cute karate shriek (hi-yaa!) that came with every chop or high kick really won our hearts over. Of course, now it's obvious that Tommy the Green Ranger was hitting that. The two have a strong chemistry and in all of their scenes together, you can cut the sexual tension with a knife… Or a Dragon Sword.

The show is so ludicrous that not only does it provide laughs; it shocks and awes you with characters who display incredible stupidity. If Rita *really* wants to destroy the Power Rangers, why not create several monsters at, make all of them grow and send them to the Power Rangers' town (Angel Grove) to wreak havoc simultaneously? And who in the hell are these brave, yet foolish souls who choose to reside in a town as horrendous as "Angel Grove"[1].

DID YOU KNOW?

- Bill the Blue Ranger (played by David Yost) is the only Power Ranger to appear in every single episode of *Mighty Morphin' Power Rangers*.
- The first 40 episodes of season one of *Mighty Morphin' Power Rangers* used stock footage from a Japanese series titled, *Zyurangers* using the fight sequences in which they are costumed.

[1]THE TOP FIVE REASONS NOT TO LIVE IN ANGEL GROVE

1. While you're walking in the park, you might be attacked by a group of clay men, donning gray spandex suits and making obnoxious, gibberish sounds.
2. There are constantly gigantic monsters battling equally massive, metal dinosaurs. They destroy streets, buildings, cars and possibly even innocent bystanders in the process.
3. Some crazy bitch (Rita Repulsa) has made a full time job out of obliterating your entire town... And she's rather persistent.
4. Your life depends on five (sometimes six) teenagers.
5. The leader of those teenagers is a face in a tube.

when playing Power Rangers, who'd you choose?

As 90s kids we often played Power Rangers with our siblings and friends. The Ranger you found yourself playing as the majority of the time says a lot about you. Read below and see your past defined in a nutshell.

GREEN RANGER: Either you had a crush on whoever was playing as the Pink Ranger or you wanted to be a leader and Red Ranger was already taken.
BLACK RANGER: You were probably black. The show itself was bold enough to blatantly make the black (or yellow) ranger their "race's color" - so kids unintentionally followed in their footsteps.
PINK RANGER: Reserved for the cutest girl. FYI, chances are whoever was the Green Ranger had a thing for you.
BLUE RANGER: They took your lunch money, had you do their homework and then worst of all, made you be the Blue Ranger. Brutal.
YELLOW RANGER: [see BLACK RANGER. Replace the word "black" with "Asian".]
RED RANGER: Congrats, you were a badass. 98% of kids wanted this role so if you got it, kudos to you. Red Ranger meant you called the shots, kicked the most imaginary butt and made the important, executive decisions - like whether to finish battling make believe Putties or stop to catch the ice cream man.

2. DOUG WAS WHIPPED.

Nickelodeon was (and still is) a **massive** part of 90s pop culture, and since *Doug* was the first *Nicktoon* ever aired, it's beyond worthy of discussing. Doug Funnie spent a good portion of his life in the 90s putting an undeserving Patti Mayonnaise on a pedestal. Obviously as adult humans, it's difficult to judge the physical attractiveness of cartoon characters – especially those who are eleven years old. That being said, Patti **is not** *that* freaking cute. She wasn't particularly smart or funny *and* she admitted to not being able to cook (in season 1, episode 11 "Doug's Cookin'"). So, what Doug saw in Miss Mayonnaise that made him go cuckoo for Cocoa Puffs, remains to be seen by the rest of us. Her raspy voice and accent were cute, but the blonde afro-esque hair, the blue and pink polka dot shirt, the lanky, gangly body and boyish charm all canceled that out.

One can make the argument that Doug isn't much of a looker himself. With that hideous green sweater vest, an enormous honker, those beady little eyes and what seemed to be some sort of balding issue (only 8 strands of hair) at such a young age, Doug wasn't exactly model material. That all being said, there's no excuse for a person to do the extremely desperate things that Doug did for Patti over the years[1].

[1]FIVE EXTREMELY DESPERATE THINGS DOUG DID FOR PATTI

1. Learned how to dance FOR PATTI.
2. Joined a school ballet FOR PATTI.
3. Handcuffed himself to Patti with no key after performing a magic trick FOR PATTI.
4. Lied about having a sick cousin to avoid going to the dance with someone other than Patti, FOR PATTI.
5. Saw a hypnotist to try to force himself to like the taste of liver and onions, which he hated, FOR PATTI.

Doug, she ain't worth it bro! There's other fish in the sea… Specifically Ariel from *The Little Mermaid*. **Way** cuter (even with the fins).

3. TGIF + SNICK = GREAT FRIDAY & SATURDAY NIGHT.

Hey, what are you doing this weekend? Wait, let me guess… You'll be doing *something* other than watching TV. It's funny because there was once a time in our lives in which we spent our weekends at home, enjoying television. Of course, the fact that we were in our youth and far below the legal drinking, clubbing or gambling ages played a part, but don't discredit *ABC's TGIF* and *Nickelodeon's SNICK*. At different times over the decade their lineups included various combinations of shows[1].

It's quite disappointing to realize that never again will a television lineup be entertaining enough to keep us home on a Friday or Saturday night. TGIF brought folks together to watch family themed sitcoms, engage with one another and enjoy some laughs. SNICK was aimed more for the kids than their parents, but it was another night of our favorite shows, jam-packed into a two hours of epic TV watching.

Reflecting on what the weekend used to mean to us in comparison to what it is now can be somewhat depressing for many. I believe this is why so many of us get ***slammered*** drunk on the weekends. Alcohol serves as a coping mechanism to block out memories of the greatness that used to be Friday & Saturday evenings. I've tried to stay home on a weekend and watch the malarkey that comes on currently and all I can say is… Stay thirsty, my friends.

[1]TGIF	SNICK
Full House	Clarissa Explains It All
Family Matters	The Ren & Stimpy Show
Perfect Strangers	Are You Afraid Of The Dark
Dinosaurs	The Adventures Of Pete & Pete
Step By Step	All That
Hangin' With Mr. Cooper	The Secret World Of Alex Mack
Boy Meets World	Kenan & Kel
Sister, Sister	Kablam!
Sabrina The Teenage Witch	Rugrats

*Not every single series to ever air on each respective block is listed above.

FUN FACT: *ABC's TGIF* **didn't stand for "Thank God It's Friday", instead the acronym meant "Thank Goodness It's Funny".**

DID YOU REALIZE **that Melissa Joan Hart was the only star of a tv series on both TGIF and SNICK with** ***Sabrina The Teenage Witch*** **and** ***Clarissa Explains It All.***

AND NOW, IT'S TIME FOR "AN ANGRY LETTER FROM 90s KIDS, TO TELEVISION NETWORKS"...

Dear Television Networks,

What in the hell are you doing lately? I mean, we understand that it's easier to make cheap, crappy reality television and poorly written shows instead of spending the money on some talented writers, and producing a more expensive studio series', but ***c'mon***. Friday night has gone from TGIF's brilliance to the place where mediocre sitcoms go to die. And Nickelodeon what's the matter with you? Replaying episodes of *That 70s Show* all day (as great as it is) won't get you higher ratings. So somebody, step up to the plate, reach into wallet, break open your piggy bank and throw together a decent block of weekend television. Until then, our attention goes to clubs, partying and booze. Good day.

Sincerely,
90s Kids.

P.S. **We're** ***really*** **starting to grow rather fond of hard liquor & the scandalousness of clubs, so get on it, time's a wastin'.**

4. UNCLE PHIL IS SHREDDER.

Nineties kids grew up on a steady diet of *Teenage Mutant Ninja Turtles* and *The Fresh Prince Of Bel-Air*, so you'd think that more people would've noticed this but we didn't! James Avery, who played Will Smith's stern yet loving Uncle Phil, also provided the voice for the Ninja Turtle's diabolical archenemy, Shredder. Who knew that after Judge Philip Banks took a bite out of crime he contributed to the problem by being an evildoing antagonist? Finding this out for the first time is quite the shocker, so hopefully you've managed to soak in that information without losing consciousness. Look **below** for some other surprising voice actor situations that took place in the 90s!

JALEEL WHITE =
SONIC THE HEDGEHOG (SONIC) &
STEVE URKEL (FAMILY MATTERS)

MARK HAMILL =
JOKER (BATMAN: THE ANIMATED SERIES) &
LUKE SKYWALKER (STAR WARS)

SCOTT WEINGER =
ALADDIN (ALADDIN) &
STEVE HALE (D.J. TANNER'S BOYFRIEND ON FULL HOUSE)

DANIEL STERN =
MARV MERCHANTS (HOME ALONE) &
KEVIN ARNOLD (NARRATOR ON THE WONDER YEARS)

5. BATMAN THE ANIMATED SERIES IS THE BEST FORM OF BATMAN.

This shouldn't really be up for debate and if you've watched *Batman The Animated Series*, surely you don't disagree. Many have tried and plenty have failed when it comes to creating Batman shows or movies. Whether you look back to the Adam West series, the Tim Burton versions, the mid-90s failures or the more recent Chris Nolan films, none can top our brilliant 90s version.

It was dark and violent, which many considered adult oriented. There were guns, punches, kicks and blood which wasn't typical for a superhero cartoon series, but 90s kids ate that up. The musical score was excellent, the animation was beautiful and the voice actors (Kevin Conroy & Mark Hamill) were damn near perfect. That's why now when someone says "Batman", most 90s kids picture *this* particular version, because it *is* Batman to them. Other movies and series' had their good and bad aspects but ultimately they contain too many issues[1] to be in the same league as the animated series. Everyone is entitled to their own opinion, but it's hard to make a case *against* the 90's animated series.[2]

[1]the issues with other forms of Batman

1. Mr. Freeze's (Arnold Schwarzenegger) idiotic puns in *Batman & Robin.*
2. George Clooney's hard nipple bat suit in *Batman & Robin.*
3. Adam West's Batman back in 1000 B.C. was fine for its time but he was lumpy and unintimidating in the bat suit. Also, he had eyebrows on his mask that were unnecessary/distracting.
4. Christian Bale's 'Batman Voice' sounds like a heavy smoker who is very, *very* constipated.
5. Marlon Wayans was cast to play Robin in *Batman Returns.* Wait, WHAT?!? Marlon Wayans is hilarious but that's so random. Marlon was even paid with a contract for two Batman films although they eventually decided not to use him.

[2]You can plead a case for other versions of Batman, unless you're fighting in Clooney's corner -- that's just preposterous.

6. REAL RELATIONSHIPS AREN'T LIKE CORY & TOPANGA'S.

The chances of a relationship surviving the winds of change that occur throughout middle school, high school and college are slim to none. But *Boy Meets World's* Cory Matthews and Topanga Lawrence managed to do the impossible, giving 90s kids foolish hope that we could do the same.

First of all, Cory and Topanga went to school and lived near each other for their entire lives – a luxury that very few have. During the show's fourth season Topanga's mother got a job in Pittsburgh, forcing her to move. In real life, this likely would've been the end of a relationship. But not on whatever world *Boy Meets World* takes place in. Instead, Topanga runs away from Pittsburgh, back to Philadelphia for her beloved Cory. Eventually her parents allowed her to live in Philly with her Aunt until her graduation, which is a bullet dodged for the happy couple.

There was also the time that Cory cheated on Topanga. It was a kiss with a girl named Lauren, who nursed Cory and his sprained ankle back to health at a ski-lodge. Not only did the lip lock take place but when Topanga questioned him about it, he lied to her. The cheat and lie combination is typically enough to get you the boot in real life but on *Boy Meets World*, it simply brought the lovers closer (after a brief breakup).

It's crucial that people remind themselves that *Boy Meets World* **is not** a documentary and Cory and Topanga's love was a one of a kind, rarer than rare, damn near unattainable connection that 99.9% of us will never experience. Sad? Maybe. True? Absolutely.

<u>fun facts about Boys Meets World</u>

1. Ben Savage (Cory) and Rider Strong (Shawn) were the only actors to appear in all 158 episodes of *Boy Meets World*.
2. Topanga is the name of a canyon in California.
3. The final line of the show was spoken by Mr. Feeny, and he said, "I love you all. Class dismissed."

7. WE MISSED OUR CHANCE TO BE ON ONE OF NICKELODEON'S GAME SHOWS.

Oh, to be a contestant on one of Nickelodeon's game shows. It was a dream that many of us had during the 90s and if you didn't fulfill it back then, you probably never will. The shows were filmed in front of a live audience at Nickelodeon Studios in Universal Studios Florida, and we wanted more than anything to be a part of one. There were a variety of different shows, each one fantastic in its own way.

WHAT WOULD YOU DO?: A classic 90s game show that was ironically hosted by the obsessive, compulsive Marc Summers. Why is that ironic? Because this was a messy game show that often had stunts involving slime, pies to the face, honey, molasses, ketchup, raw eggs, peanut butter and any other sticky, gooey substance that many OCD sufferers consider cringe worthy. The audience members of this show were also used as its contestants, making it one of the most appealing shows to attend. There wasn't a *What Would You Do?* fan in the world who didn't want an opportunity to choose a door on the "Wall O' Stuff"[1].

DOUBLE DARE: Guess what? *Double Dare* was also hosted by Marc Summers and it was equally if not more messy than *What Would You Do?* For a guy with OCD, Summers sure had a knack for finding the most messily sticky, slime filled shows. The competitions were a combination of trivia questions and physical challenges where teams went head to head in some super sloppy activities which added to the shows appeal.

FIGURE IT OUT: The host, Summer Sanders was easy on the eyes which only benefited the show. The concept of *Figure It Out* was to pit a kid with unique talents or special achievements (I use the words talents & achievements *very* loosely) against a panel of four Nickelodeon celebrities who tried to guess the contestants skill. And I'm using the word "skill" loosely as well (see *figure 7.1*). Many of us wanted to be on the show and put our abilities or gifts on display, but the fact that the prizes consisted of things like crappy bicycles and *Figure It Out* messenger bags wasn't enough to get us off the couch.

NICK ARCADE: Just about every 90s kid would've loved to be on *Nick Arcade*. It consisted of 30 second video game competitions and some trivia that led to an epic "virtual video game" ending. The show seemed to seek out the worst gamers alive, making us cringe as we watched them fail at simple tasks (e.g. collecting rings on *Sonic*). "The Video Zone" was and still is a dream of mine because who wouldn't *love* to participate in a live action video game? For years many of us wondered how the hell those kids managed to get *inside* of a video game, unaware of the simplicity of a green screen.

NICKELODEON GUTS: Mike O'Malley was a fantastic host for this show that was geared toward the athletic type. The competitions on this series looked mighty difficult as a kid. Hell, they had legitimate young athletes battling it out in a bunch of crap that I don't think I'm capable of doing *now*. Remember the friggin' Aggro Crag? It was a giant, fabricated mountain that contestants raced to the top of, activating targets along the way. In retrospect, this is quite possibly the most difficult kid's game show of all time. That being said, it would've been an absolute blast to partake in the festivities, even if my physical capabilities were subpar.

WILD AND CRAZY KIDS: Omar Gooding, Donnie Jeffcoat and Jessica Gaynes (Annette Chavez in the first season) hosted *Wild and Crazy Kids*. It featured large teams of children competing in physical challenges. It looked like tons of fun ***and*** an opportunity to meet Cuba Gooding Jr.'s bro, why wouldn't you want in? Plus, they had some pretty sweet celebrity appearances[2] occasionally.

LEGENDS OF THE HIDDEN TEMPLE: The Silver Snakes, Blue Barracudas, Purple Parrots, Orange Iguanas, Green Monkeys and Red Jaguars battled it out in three rounds of epic competition in the temple. It consisted of answering questions and performing physical stunts until one team prevailed, earning them the chance to go through the temple and retrieve an artifact within three minutes for the grand prize. Sounds simple enough, right? Wrong! There were temple guards that not only scared the living sh*t out of the viewers at home, but delayed the contestants' Temple Run. In addition, it became painfully frustrating to watch when some of those kids struggled to put the statue in the "Shrine of the Silver Monkey" together. It was THREE freaking pieces that fit the *exact* same way *every* single episode! Surely these dodoes had watched *Legends of the Hidden Temple* before being on it, so they had to have ample time to prepare and plan for the statue.

[1]A wall of 20 numbered doors, each containing a prize (t-shirt, gym bag, etc.) or unpleasant surprise (pie to the face, whipped cream squirted in the face).

[2] Hulk Hogan, Chuck Norris, Arnold Schwarzenegger, Jonathon Taylor Thomas, Lark Voorhies and a *young* Tobey Maguire.

figure 7.1

SOME OF THE WORST *FIGURE IT OUT* CONTESTANTS:

1. A kid who could bite a piece of cheese into the shape of Florida. Are you f*cking kidding me? At least learn all 50 states, dude.
2. A boy who collected his toe jam and turned it into a ball. Assembling dead skin, sock fuzz and sweat into a ball of funk is disgusting and not skillful in the least bit. Did this kid know about baseball cards? Collections of those have potential to be worth something and they don't smell like hate.
3. A kid who could bend fingers back and make them touch wrist. It's called being double jointed, *not* talented.
4. A kid who discovered that peanut shells hide the scent of pig urine. How and why he stumbled upon this brilliant breakthrough - we may never know. Nor will we want to.
5. A kid who stuck lobsters to eyelids and tongue. Really? I mean, *reeeeally*?
6. A kid who collected human hair to make dolls. I would say something rather negative about 'em but this destined voodoo doll maker might steal one of my luscious locks and lead me to my demise.
7. A kid with a rattail down his neck. Wait, they gave out prizes for rocking ridiculous hair fads?

8. BLOWING INTO CARTRIDGES IS THE GREATEST QUICK FIX EVER.

CTRL + Z, the morning after pill, tape, whiteout, glue – those are some of the world's easiest quick fixers. As impressive as they may be, nothing is as effortless and remarkable as simply blowing into a malfunctioning video game cartridge. That's right, back in the day when a video game froze or wasn't properly working we didn't panic. All it took was a huff, a puff and a blow into the cartridge, then presto! It magically worked just fine. This was an era in which no Blu-Ray disc, DVD or any other digitally composed video games were being distributed. Our games were presented on a blocky hunk of plastic that was stuffed full of computer chips. Whenever these cartridges acted up in anyway, our instincts told us to blow into them and for whatever reason, it worked. Nowadays, if your game is damaged you're simply out of luck because they are all created on some type of disc, making this method obsolete. When 90s kids' games broke we blew, in present times when a game breaks it just sucks.

a tip for kids nowadays: Try blowing on your *Call Of Duty* disc when it's scratched, see if it works any better... (heads up, it won't).

9. THE NEW GENERATION HAS MADE THE ICE CREAM MAN A RARITY.

Do y'all remember the good ol' days when you didn't have to find the ice cream man **because the ice cream man found you**? And when he arrived, you browsed the smorgasbord of frozen treats thinking long and hard before settling on one of those frosty delicacies. Don't you miss that? (Not just the tasty ice cream but the times when your hardest decision of the day was "Drumstick or Ice Cream Sandwich?") Well get used to reminiscing because the lazy asses in Generation Z have so much technology that the majority of 'em won't be going outside unless it's to check the mail for their latest Netflix arrivals. Simply put, the new generation opts to sit inside of the house browsing the web, playing video games and watching absurd amounts of television, rendering the ice cream man useless. No more delicious Ninja Turtles Ice Cream Bar with bubble gum eyes, no more Flintstone Push Ups, no more Choco Tacos, etc. Sad day, thank those *Drake & Josh* watching, Justin Bieber loving fatties[1].

[1]Anyone else see the hypocrisy in me calling Generation Y "fatties" for ruining my easy access to ice cream?

10. BAD PARENTS + CURIOUS KIDS = *RUGRATS*.

Rugrats was always a superb cartoon and a fan favorite, mainly because most of the episodes featured the group of babies going on some type of dangerous (at least in their imagination) adventure. Why were they constantly exploring places they had no business going? Because their parents were just **the worst**. It's a miracle these babies managed to stay alive. It's an even bigger wonder how Child Protective Services never made an appearance during the series. Every character on this toon was just that, a *character* – often resulting in a bad combination of inattentive adult mixed with explorative toddler. Let's evaluate each individual and understand in detail, why things were so hectic.

the parents

HOWARD & BETTY DEVILLE: Phil & Lil's parents who were complete opposites. Howard said no more than four words over all his appearances in the series while Betty was obnoxiously loud. Not only did she not have an inside voice, but she was dropping her twins off at the Pickles' home *way* too often. Like, pretty much every episode, often.

CHAZ FINSTER: Chuckie's single dad, Chaz was somewhat of a timid, wimpy man and he raised his boy to be quite similar. In Chaz's defense, he had lost his wife (revealed in a depressing episode titled, "*Mothers Day*"), and he was a very loving father. Unfortunately, like Howard & Betty he made the mistake of dropping Chuckie off at the Pickles' home, where they do everything but supervise the kids.

CHARLOTTE & DREW PICKLES: Oh, man – where to begin with these two. You had Charlotte who was a workaholic, loud, abrasive, mildly condescending woman that *always* had her cell phone to her ear, even when she wasn't at work. Then there was Drew, who was a complete and utter pushover. Supposedly he was the father but it always seemed as if his daughter, Angelica, was the man of the house.

The little cookie loving brat acted like a child of the corn and instead of being the stern voice of authority, Drew used terms of endearment[1] when talking to Angelica.

DIDI & STU PICKLES: Stu was a loving and caring father which was a plus, but he spent a good 80% of his time in the basement. It was down there that he worked countless hours for his own company, *Pickles Toys*. Stu was convinced that each of his toy inventions would be the one to "put Pickles Toys on the map". For Tommy, the downside of his father often being busy was worth it since he got to test out every new toy. Didi on the other hand is a nice mother and actually wants to be a good parent so much that it hurt her. She was so consumed with reading books and listening to parental advice from child psychologist, Dr. Lipschitz, that she didn't ever notice when her son had wandered off on an adventure.

the children

PHIL & LIL DEVILLE: These two were a hair bow away from being indistinguishable. They enjoyed eating worms, which they never would've tasted had a decent supervisor been around. They also bickered and argued a lot, using each other's full names, Phillip and Lillian during these verbal spats.

CHUCKIE FINSTER: This kid was such a buzz killing downer. Pessimistic thoughts and negative words, spewed from his mouth while he shot down potential adventures with his catchphrase, "Maybe this isn't such a good idea." On top of his gloomy outlook on things, Chuckie was afraid of damn near everything. Clowns, the dark and the "guy on the oatmeal box with the scary hat", just to name a few. One can make an argument that Chuckie is the biggest chicken-sh*t of all time, or the bravest soul alive for always being loyal and facing his fears during the groups adventures. And in his defense, sometimes *Rugrats* gave legit reasons to be scared[2].

ANGELICA PICKLES: This was one mean spirited little girl. Behavior like Angelica's should warrant counseling, a spanking or possibly even an exorcism. This spoiled brat antagonized the other four babies for no reason other than to be evil. She was rude, crude and socially unacceptable which is why her best (and only) friend was a doll named Cynthia.

TOMMY PICKLES: The greatest leader of the 90s (as voted on www.Things90sKidsRealize.com), Tommy Pickles is quite a badass. The little dude kept a screwdriver in his diaper that he used to escape his playpen and go on quests. He stared fear in the eyes without blinking on multiple occasions. Countless times he led these babies on adventures, into trouble and back out of trouble with the intestinal fortitude and bravery of a soldier. You'd think an adventurous baby like Tommy needed supervision but he handled his own business, like a boss.

[1]Terms like "angel", "princess", "muffin", "pumpkin", etc.

[2] The episode where Angelica dreams she's having a baby brother was terrifying. He was giant and chased her around wanting to eat her like a snack. The other "sleep with the lights on" moment was when Chaz dreamed that he put Chuckie to bed. He walks into the living room and sees Stu standing there with his back to him. Chaz says "Stu! I didn't know you were coming over." The figure turns around – giant eyes, a goofy face and creepily exclaims, "I'm not Stu!" as Chaz screams and the episode ends.

11. WE HAD BRILLIANT CHILDREN'S BOOK SERIES'.

For every child who enjoyed reading there were two disgruntled kids who were irritated by the thought of a paperback. Whether you weren't so fond of literature or you jumped for joy when it was "DEAR" (drop everything and read) time in class, chances are you found something you thoroughly enjoyed in our awesome selection of books that were popular in the 1900s.

Berenstein Bears: While these books were created in the '60s, they gained massive popularity and published most of their titles during the '80s and '90s – so we can claim the hell out of 'em. Bear Country was one of those fictional places that you always wanted to visit. Each book taught some type of lesson, e.g. watching too much TV, eating too much junk food, getting in fights, etc. As creative as the books were, the literal names of the characters (*Mama Bear, Papa Bear, Brother Bear & Sister Bear*) weren't so impressive. Regardless of the disappointingly generic bear names, the books were beautifully illustrated, educational and heartening.

Choose Your Own Adventures: Easily one of the most creative concepts of the 90s, these things were about as close to a video game as a book can possibly be. You were the star of the show taking action into your own hands and making decisions that eventually decided the story's outcome. The goal was to make the best choices and have a happy ending but we can't deny how enjoyable it was to fail miserably and meet your demise in some horrific fashion.

Where's Waldo?: Ok, so it was only pictures but it was bound together and you turned its pages so I'm calling it a book! Scanning these illustrations in search of the red and white striped shirt wearing Waldo was one of our favorite pastimes and it became a pop culture phenomenon.

Goosebumps: For many of us, R.L. Stine's Goosebumps series was our first time experiencing the "horror" genre. The stories managed to be steadily entertaining but they weren't really *that* terrifying on a regular basis. Some of the concepts were preposterous, even for an easy scare or a seven year old. That being said, Goosebumps books were highly successful because whatever they cooked, we ate right up regardless of how unfathomable it was.

Judy Blume Books: Her work was geared more towards girls but boy did she have some that appealed to everyone, regardless of their gender. *Superfudge* and *Freckle Juice* for example, were loved by the masses. This woman was truly in tune with her young female readers, writing relatable stories for them, regarding a broad range of topics from bullying, to teen sex.

Hank The Cowdog: A series of novels that revolved around a cocky cowdog with a knack for finding sticky situations. Now, from that description it may sound somewhat ridiculous but rest assured, it's over 50 books worth of brilliance. It was actually created in the early eighties but had great popularity amongst 90s kids that enjoyed reading about a dog who was the "Head of Security" on a ranch in Texas.

Sideways Stories From Wayside School: A trilogy of books written by Louis Sachar and read by 90s kids across the globe. The books told several stories about a school built 30 stories high, with one room per story and for some odd reason, no 19th story at all. These were great reads because all of the characters were zany screwballs.

12. KENAN & KEL WERE THE BEST 90s COMEDY DUO.

If you watched *All That* then you should remember how hilarious any of the pieces involving Kenan Thompson or Kel Mitchell were! Do you recall Kenan in the sketch titled: "*Everyday French With Pierre Escargot*"? It revolved around boy wearing a raincoat, sitting in a bath tub, blabbering French gibberish, before giving the ridiculous English translation of what he had just said. It never failed to draw a good chuckle. Or Kel's "*Repair Man"* skit in which a piece of equipment would break and Kel (as Repair Man) would come crashing through the ceiling or wall, claiming he could fix it. Then he proceeded to make the damage worse and destroy damn near everything in sight, making people furious. The best part was when he was asked to identify himself, he gave the catchphrase, "I'm, Repair man, man, man, man, man, man", followed up by a menacing laugh. *Classic.*

Their humor transferred over when they starred in *Kenan & Kel* together. It delivered everything we wanted in a show and they played well off of each other. Kel was the accident prone, orange soda loving goober, while Kenan fulfilled the role of adventure seeking, trouble finding teenager. Their chemistry was fantastic on television as well as the big screen when they made *Good Burger*. The film had Kel perfectly playing the role of Ed, an idiotic employee, and when you mixed in Kenan's easily annoyed character, Dexter, a 90s kid cult classic is what you got. Kenan and Kel will forever be the decade's favorite comedy duo.

five fun facts:

1. *Kenan & Kel* ran for 4 seasons (62 episodes).
2. Kel provided the voice for T-Bone in the children's cartoon series, *Clifford the Big Red Dog.*
3. Kel appeared in Kanye West's 2004 music video for the song, "All Falls Down".
4. Kenan ranked #88 on VH1's list of 100 Greatest Teen Stars.
5. Kenan joined the cast of *Saturday Night Live* in 2003. He was the first *SNL* cast member to be born after the shows premiere in 1975.

13. JUICE MAKERS WANTED US TO DIE OF DEHYDRATION.

The makers of *Kool-Aid Bursts*, *CapriSun**, *Hi-C*, *Juicy Juice* and seemingly every other brand of juice must have decided that they wanted to kill all of the 90s kids via dehydration. While they came in an assortment of forms such as bottles, boxes and pouches, they shared one commonality: They provided a highly insufficient amount of juice. Typically when a person becomes thirsty, they require more than two sips of drink to quench that feeling. But for whatever reason, that was the unsatisfying dosage we received from those companies. As delicious as their drinks were, it just wasn't enough.

We all knew that kid who brought 2-3 boxes of juice to lunch on the regular because he knew one *Juicy Juice* just wasn't going to cut it. These are the trials and tribulations of any 90s kid who suffered through the packed lunch experience. And what's really shocking is that after all these years, not a single company has altered the dimensions of their juice holder – continuing to deliver the bare minimum. By the looks of things, juice makers are satisfied with serving inadequate amounts of liquid to this next generation as well.

***sidenote:** Capri Sun gets an extra verbal lashing because they provided us with a thin yellow straw that had to be jimmied into a tiny, resistant hole with the utmost precision. Failure to do so resulted in a sticky mess that makes you question whether or not the juice was worth the squeeze.

14. LA GEAR MADE THE SWEETEST SNEAKERS EVER.

Oh, LA Lights. Let me start by reminding you that these shoes lit up. THEY F****** LIT UP! When you were a kid, anything that wasn't a lamp and still managed to light up was automatically labeled "da bomb". If you were wearing these sneakers at their peak popularity, then you were feeling *pretty* confident on the playground. Unfortunately the stuff making these epic zapatos work their magic consisted of mercury which led to their eventual demise. It's a shame really, but until someone invents a shoe that dispenses ice cream sandwiches and plays clips from the *Space Jam* soundtrack every time a step is taken, the LA Lights will be second to ***none.***

10 other awesome 90s things that didn't survive the test of time...

1. Surge Soda
2. Rice Krispie Treats Cereal
3. Oreo O's Cereal
4. Butterfinger BBs
5. 3D Doritos
6. Ninja Turtles Pies (with green filling)
7. S'more's Lunchables
8. Sprinkle Spangles
9. Cheetos Paws
10. French Toast Crunch (In the USA)

15. WE SPENT COUNTLESS HOURS PLAYING VARIOUS FORMS OF MARIO AND SONIC GAMES.

Sonic The Hedgehog and *Super Mario* are two of the most beloved video game franchises of all-time, for very good reason. Sonic was amazing to play as a kid because you got to control a character who was moving speedily through slopes, high drops and loop-de-loops while jumping on springs and collecting rings in the process. Of course we all hated stepping on spikes or running into an enemy and having our hard earned rings shoot out all over the place.

In *Sonic the Hedgehog 2* when Sonic's useless, obnoxious, pain in the ass sidekick Tails was introduced, the majority of us hated him. If anything Tails slowed down your play and made you despise any sidekick that wasn't named Luigi. Despite Tails sucking at just about everything, the games are still classics that remain beyond fun to play to this day.

Mario allowed us the chance to take control of a stumpy, overweight Italian man with a mustache like Tom Selleck, and run him through courses, obstacles and obnoxious Goombas and Koopa Troopers. The fun always went up a couple notches when you acquired one of the additional powers (super mushrooms, fire flowers, raccoon suit, feather/cape, etc.).

Over the years we got to play as Luigi, ride Yoshi and of course, save Princess Toadstool/ Peach's kidnap prone self a number of times. One magnificent part of the Mario franchise is that it led to the creation of *Super Mario Kart* which is the bee's knees. This isn't just any racing game! The ability to get "power-up" items (e.g. shells, mushrooms, bananas, etc.) created the potential to change the leader of any race in an instant. Launching objects at other cars or leaving a slippery surprise that would cause then to spin out while you cruised right past 'em was what *Super Mario Kart* was all about. It was addictive, incredible and the sole reason why still we don't trust our vehicles to drive over banana peels.

While these were easily the two most popular franchises of the 1990s, they are actually more than that. To this day there are games being created based on these characters and they remain highly successful. The blue hedgehog and overweight, Italian plumber are pioneers in the video game world, that are seemingly here to stay forever.

RANDOM THOUGHTS:

1. Do you remember the music that played during the Sonic The Hedgehog games when you were drowning? Scariest piece of music, **ever** composed. Strikes fear deep into our souls to this day.

2. Rainbow Road on *Super Mario Kart* was for bad asses only. Guard rails? Who needed 'em? That level was one of the biggest challenges of our first 15 years of life.

16. MUFASA'S DEATH WAS THE FIRST TRAGEDY OF OUR LIVES.

For a character that only survived part of the film, Mufasa made a quick impression on everyone who ever saw *The Lion King*. Perhaps it was the way he led as King of Pride Rock, or maybe it was James Earl Jones' soothing voice that drew us to him. Either way, watching Mufasa be killed by a stampede was one of the most traumatizing experiences of many 90s kids' lives. A shocking death such as this one is rare because it's a children's movie and typically the good people don't die, but Disney had something different in mind with The Lion King.

When it happened some of us shed a tear or two (*hundred*), while others went into month long depressions. One thing that is universally agreed upon on the same level is that we ***HATE*** Scar with a burning passion. We didn't forgive him then, we don't forgive him now, nor will we ever. To this day the mere sight of his face ignites fury in our bones. I think it's only right that this discussion is ended with a phrase that we felt as children, even if we didn't know the right words to express our feelings quite yet: **"F*CK YOU SCAR."**

WHO ELSE thought it sounded like they were saying the phrase, "Pink pajamas, penguins on the bottom", during *The Circle of Life* song. I know that I'm not alone on this.

17. OREGON TRAIL WAS THE BEST PART OF ELEMENTARY SCHOOL.

For some reason parents and teachers thought it was a good idea to use this game as an educational tool. Was it? Well let's see, do you remember any of the landmarks shown in the game? No. What about the historical figures or the information given by random settlers encountered along the trail? Negative. We don't recall anything other than the raw, gritty part of traveling such as shooting buffalo, visiting trading posts and wagon mates dying one after the other in a variety of unique fashions – so perhaps we really did learn something, even if it wasn't what the adults intended for us to take from *Oregon Trail*. However, so much time spent playing this game has given 90s kids the traveling confidence of a 19th century pioneer. Leave us in the wilderness with a bottle of water, some mixed nuts and an ox and we'll survive. The kids nowadays can't walk two blocks without the GPS on their cell phones.

18. ARNOLD HAD A PSYCHO STALKER NAMED HELGA PATAKI.

The children of P.S. 118 on *Hey Arnold!* were only in the 4th grade, but Helga Pataki's passionate obsession with Arnold was beyond the average kiddy crush. If Arnold knew the potential danger he was in every time he hung around Helga, a restraining order likely would have been intact. This isn't an exaggeration either; the list of things Helga did over the years is alarming, and sometimes quite frightening.

things that Arnold's psycho, stalker Helga Pataki did.

1. Dated *Stinky* in an attempt to make Arnold jealous.
2. Carved Arnold's name into trees.
3. Attempted to sabotage Arnold's date with a girl named Lila, following the two around. She drilled holes in a love boat and turned the speed up on the rides *all* to ruin Lila's experience.
4. Pretended to be Arnold's pen pal and faked a French accent just to go on a date with him.
5. Created a shrine that included a bubble gum statue of Arnold's head.

In Helga's defense, she was living in a very dysfunctional household. Her father, "Big Bob" was a douche bag, pager salesman who paid her little to no attention and clearly loved his other daughter Olga more. Olga was "*Little Miss Perfect*" but that's no reason to put Helga and her unibrow on the backburner. To make matters worse Helga's mother is so obviously an alcoholic. She was drunk *all the time*. The woman was constantly slurring her words while she made and consumed her spiked "smoothies" before falling asleep in the most random of places. If that isn't enough evidence of a drinking problem, she had a license revoked and was required to do some type of community service at one point, which sounds a lot like Mrs. Pataki earned herself a DUI. Being part of a family like that sounds rough, especially for a 4th grader but does that really justify Helga's borderline psychopath actions? Criminy, no!

19. WE HAD PRO WRESTLING AT ITS BEST.

There was no decade better for professional wrestling and its fans than the 1990s. The different brands, the rating wars, the wrestlers and the wrestling itself were all superior to the current product being manufactured by Vince McMahon & company.

NEW GENERATION: Basically this was the era that lured most of us into watching wrestling. Labeled "new generation", it was the period in which some of the greatest wrestlers of all time flourished. There was **Shawn Michaels,** the dancing, flashy heartbreak kid who delivered "Sweet Chin Music" to his opponents. **The Undertaker**, who many of us got chills watching as he played the role of "dead man". He gained energy from his Urn, tombstone pile drove his opponents to defeat and rolled his eyes into the back of his head, fully satisfying the visual effects of his gimmick. **"Big Daddy Cool" Diesel**, the leather wearing monster put on some of the most entertaining matches of the decade while also managing to be longest reigning *WWF* champion of the 1990s. **Razor Ramon** was the *Scareface* type character who always had a toothpick in his mouth and said the phrase, "Say hello to the bad guy." He'd call guys "chico", flick a toothpick in their face and then kick their ass on a regular basis. Razor is arguably the greatest superstar to never win the *WWF Championship*. Last but not least was **Bret "The Hitman" Hart** who is arguably the greatest technical wrestler to ever lace 'em up. Many agree with his slogan that claimed to be "The best there is, the best there was and the best there ever will be." Bret Hart *and* the "New Generation" era ended as a whole at *Survivor Series 1997* when the infamous "Montreal Screw Job" took place[1].

ATTITUDE ERA: In 1997 when the WWF began losing money, wrestlers (*Kevin Nash, Scott Hall, Psycho Sid to name a few*) and ratings to WCW, they made drastic, yet revolutionary changes in the sports entertainment world. Basically they increased the cussing, violence and scantily clad women, then developed storylines with more drama and excitement to provide a "shock factor". **Stone Cold Steve Austin** was the head of the snake, throwing middle fingers, drinking beer and having an epic feud with **Vince McMahon**, who went from being a laid back commenter to the corrupt, ruthless, a-hole owner. **The Rock's** popularity began to rise during this stretch as well. His marvelous skills on the microphone combined with his wrestling abilities and catchphrases that fans chanted along with him resulted in one of the most popular superstars since Hulk Hogan. **Degeneration X** was the group of misfits that ran around breaking rules and telling people to "suck it". Led by **Shawn Michaels** originally, **Triple H** took over after Michaels, and ended up developing into a future hall of famer himself. Add in **The Undertaker** still kicking ass and doing evil deeds, plus **Mankind (Mick Foley)** taking brutal beatings in matches like *Hell In a Cell* and you've got the most badass era of wrestling you'll ever see.

[1] A controversial, real life event in which *WWF* owner Vince McMahon went back on his word to Bret Hart during the main event of a Pay-Per-View, in Hart's home country of Canada. A secret manipulation of the match's ending result was devised by McMahon and discussed ahead of time with Hart's opponent, Shawn Michaels. Vince decided that Shawn Michaels would win the match *and* the WWF Title from Hart, by any means necessary. The plan that was executed consisted of Shawn putting Bret in the "Sharp Shooter" (a submission move) and Vince ordering the match's referee, Earl Hebner to call for the bell as if Bret Hart had submitted. Michaels was declared the victor and crowned as the new WWF Champion while a furious Bret Hart, jumped ship to rival company, *WCW*.

20. OUR SPIDER-MAN & X-MEN CARTOONS WERE BETTER THAN THEIR MOVIE VERSIONS.

The *Spider-Man* animated series was watered down by censorship yet it found a way to be great. No punching of the bad guys, no use of the word "kill", and the fact that they strayed away from the comics were all ingredients that had potential to ruin the cartoon, yet they didn't! There was a ton of attention paid to Mary Jane and Peter Parker's mushy, gushy love story which could've been detrimental to the entertainment level of this show as well, *but it wasn't*. The awesomeness might have had something to do with the fact that the show featured all of the classic *Spider-Man* villains such as: **Kingpin, Doctor Octopus, Scorpion, Green Goblin, Mysterio, The Vulture, Shocker, The Rhino, The Hobgoblin, Venom, Carnage and The Chameleon**. The movies weren't awful and there was a lot of promise for the Spider-Man legacy, especially after the first. But *Spider-Man 2* was so-so and *Spider-Man 3* was a catastrophic, massacre that made us want to shoot web in our eyeballs, pull 'em from the sockets and run back to 1994 to relive our beloved Spidey.

As for *X-Men* they never failed to deliver the goods. The storylines made a conscious effort to incorporate the comics into them, whereas the movies steered away from that, doing their own thing. The animated version of *X-Men* offered a balanced attack, providing a little bit of everything. You had brilliant storylines, plenty of fight sequences and a good amount of humor – especially when Wolverine and Cyclops had their verbal spats. Rogue was as attractive as a cartoon can possibly be, Gambit was a badass and the other characters played well off of each other. One of the few things that transferred to both the cartoon and movie was the universal feeling that Cyclops is a douche. If Wolverine hates you, then so does everybody else. In closing, it needs to be said that Wolverine crying in each movie version of the *X-Men* trilogy **and** *X-Men Origins* was unacceptable. It's friggin' Wolverine, he's supposed to be a borderline animal. Wolverine + Crying = **NOT OK**.

21. WE CREATED "TEEN POP PRINCESSES".

It's unclear if this is something to be proud or ashamed of, but either way it began with us. Nowadays people like Miley Cyrus, Miranda Cosgrove and Demi Lovato exist because of the 90s pop princesses who paved the way for them in our decade. The big four (who all graced us with their presence in the late 90s) are laid out for your reminiscing pleasures below.

Britney Spears: The head of the Teen Pop Princess snake is and always will be Britney Spears. In January of 1999 her debut album, *Baby One More Time* opened at #1 on the U.S. Billboard 200 and she's been an icon ever since. Anyone with ears heard "Baby One More Time" and "Oops I Did It Again (*reading the titles of those songs alone will have them stuck in your head for the next few hours*). Those of us who possessed television saw the classic music video with Britney in a schoolgirl uniform countless times and she gained a massive following, whether it was for her voice or her physical attractiveness.

Christina Aguilera: In August of 1999 her self titled album *Christina Aguilera* was released, filling our ears with those amazing vocals. Hits included "Genie In A Bottle", "What A Girl Wants", and "Come On Over Baby". While Aguilera *easily* has the best voice of all the teen pop princesses, she tends to over sing and it can be a little much. And by "a little much", I mean it just gets obnoxious. Don't get me wrong, her range is surreal but how annoying is it when she does that "***Wo-oh-ohhhh-whoa-heeeyy-ayeaaaaaah***" thing?

Jessica Simpson: She had an album named *Sweet Kisses* and a popular single titled, "I Wanna Love You Forever" which was likely the first time most of us heard her. Simpson's music was high on the charts but not quite Britney or Christina's level. Hell, some don't recognize Jessica Simpson because of her music from the 1990s so much as her marriage & divorce from Nick Lachey, her "cute" dimwittedness and her bad movies during the 2000s.

<u>Mandy Moore:</u> Mandy toured with *NSYNC in 1999 and had a debut album named *So Real* that was released in December of that year. Moore was the least popular of the main pop princesses, her album peaking at #31 on the U.S. Billboard 200. To this day she's remained wholesome, never making any music or videos that were too provocative or taking any scantily clad photos.

22. SCHOLASTIC BOOK ORDERS WERE... EXCITING?

This is one of the most confusing childhood tendencies ever! It's a concept that scientists around the globe (*Bill-Nye* included) should be researching to come up with explanations for. The thought of kids, who generally speaking, don't like to read being *so* enthusiastic and excited about ordering from a catalog that serves strictly reading material, is a concept that bamboozles everyone, ourselves included.

When teachers handed out those flimsy, yet precious **Scholastic Book Orders** there was no fighting the urge to splurge. Sure we could've purchased these books at any retailer, but *it just wasn't the same*. See, doing it through the catalog meant you'd make **your own choices** and your parents, encouraged by your desire to read were likely to approve of your selections, then sign and seal a nice little check that you'd deliver to school. It was the one decision that we really got to make for ourselves. Sure we couldn't watch certain shows or movies, and we weren't allowed to eat cereal for all three meals of the day but, we were making executive decisions when it came to selecting books from Scholastic.

The following weeks would consist of a lack of focus as we waited eagerly for those heaps of books to be mailed to us. The level of anticipation was high and then finally... Delivery day came. You'd get your order in a nice little stack and at that moment, life was **great**. Then you'd get home and realize you had no interest in masses of children's literature. All of a sudden your pogs, Giga Pets and action figures looked **slightly** more entertaining than Judy Blume's novels.

sidenote: Pizza Hut's "Book It!" program was a tricky way to get kids to read. Read a book, get a free pizza. Adults knew we'd do anything for a free pizza and they used that to their advantage.

23. *ARE YOU AFRAID OF THE DARK?* LEGITIMATELY SCARED US.

When the "Midnight Society" gathered to tell tales of horror and fright on *Are You Afraid Of The Dark*?, we all turned into scaredy-cats. Upon reflection, some of those episodes and characters were too over the top to be considered scary. But then, there were the other installments in which they created some of the most fear-provoking, terrifying crap known to 90s kids.

Rick Hagerty: He was a teenager that died and in ghost form, haunted his best friend, Mike Buckley in an episode called, *"The Tale of the Shiny Red Bicycle."* Very disturbing stuff, to say the least.

Alternate Dimension Black Figures: In *"The Tale of the Silver Specs"*, a kid would put on some glasses and creatures covered in black cloth appeared. As a result, we hesitate to put on 3D specs to this day.

The Lonely Ghost Girl: In *"The Tale of the Lonely Ghost"*, this weird, mute ghost girl wrote eerie things on the walls of her room. **Not cool.**

A Creepy Ass Doll: *"The Tale of the Dark Music" featured* creepy ass music that would play before a creepy ass doll would come out of a creepy ass closet. Creepy ass episode.

Madeline: This spine-chilling old lady from *"The Tale Of Apartment 214"* haunted a poor girl for failing to follow through on visiting her. Nobody likes a flake but *haunting* seems like a stiff penalty for bailing on plans. This episode left many petrified of elderly folks.

The Frozen Ghost: All I need to say are these two words: "I'm cold." That alone should remind you of what was quite possibly the most bloodcurdling moment in the history of *Are You Afraid Of The Dark?* During the episode *"The Tale Of The Frozen Ghost"* there is a part where a ghost boy who comes out during the wintery times appears and whispers "I'm cold" in an extremely spooky fashion. Many 90s kids ruined clean pairs of underwear when this episode proceeded to scare the crap out of us.

All in all, the show was generally capable of delivering a solid fright to plenty of 90s kids. Come to think of it, we never had a shortage of terrors growing up as *Are You Afraid of the Dark*, *Goosebumps*, and *Scary Stories To Tell In The Dark* provided us with a hefty supply of scary junk.

24. CLASSROOM GAMES WERE MORE FOR OUR LAZY TEACHERS THAN FOR US.

At the time we were so happy to be doing anything other then learning that we didn't really detect just how un-educational classroom games were. Sure, a quick activity every few weeks isn't going to be a setback but there were teachers who legitimately made "Heads Up, Seven Up" a part of their lesson plan. Maybe you'll recall some of these fun but unproductive blasts from the past:

***Heads Up, Seven Up:** **The best of all classroom games, the teacher said those four precious words, "heads down, thumbs up" and it began. Seven lucky souls walked around the room pressing down the thumb of one of their classmates. Once seven thumbs had been pressed down, those individuals had the opportunity to guess who the culprit was. Of course you were unlikely to guess correctly, unless you snuck a peek of the person's shoes (which a good 94% of us did).**

*This game was a good opportunity to press the thumb of the girl or boy you had a crush on. Subtle, but it let 'em know they were on your radar.

***Silent Ball:** **Everyone hushed their mouths and sat on their desks, tossing a ball around. Speaking, throwing a bad pass or dropping a good one got you eliminated. The last kid standing, or I suppose *sitting* on top of their desk claimed victory. Little did we know, the real winner was the teacher who had no curriculum and pure silence.**

*This was another good opportunity to let that special someone know that you were thinking about them, by strictly passing the ball to them.

Around The World: Two students went head to head. The teacher would display a flash card, usually a math question. Whoever answered first advanced to the next opponent. The one on one tournament structure for this game was like Mortal Kombat minus the violence, blood, gore and fatalities, plus some math questions. The student who made it all the way around the class was declared winner. This game was easily the most educational of them all.

Hot Or Cold: A student leaves the room, the teacher hides an object, the student returns and searches. The rest of the class gives the hunter guidance by saying "cold", "cool", "warm" or "hot". This provided suspense and plenty of laughs over the years.

The Quiet Game: In retrospect, this isn't even a game. Nor is it subtle or clever. This is the teacher getting their students to shut up by telling 'em whoever stays quiet the longest wins. What schemers our teachers were, huh?

25. FAMILY MATTERS? NOT TO THE WINSLOWS!

Remember those commercials from the 90s that asked parents, "It's 10pm, do you know where your children are?" If Harriet and Carl Winslow had a chance to answer that, the response probably would've been somewhere along the lines of "No, nor do we care." Judy, the Winslow's youngest child on *Family Matters* was there for plenty of episodes and then one day, she wasn't. Why? Nobody knows! She's not a figment of your imagination either; there are four seasons worth of footage that proves her existence. How can a daughter and sister vanish in thin air and nobody speaks a word about it? Unforgivable, Winslow family, **un-for-givable**.

Completely allowing a daughter to vanish wasn't the only poor parenting we saw. For years, Carl and Harriet allowed Laura to be a grade A, snobby, rude and more importantly -- ***shallow***, brat. Steve Urkel spent years doing his damndest to please Laura and she walked all over him. Then, when he wore a sports coat, removed the bifocals and put a twist on his name (Stefan Urquelle) she was all over him. Laura was superficial and highly overrated by Urkel. It's not like she wasn't a pretty girl, but the fact that Steve completely passed on Myra Monkhouse constantly to continue pursuing Laura was frustrating to watch! The guy had a smokin' hot girl who was far more interested in him yet he blew her off *for Laura*? As thick as that man's glasses were, he should've been able to see how poor his decisions were as clearly as the rest of us did.

FUN FACT: Jaimee Foxworth, who played Judy Winslow had a brief stint in the adult film industry under the name, **Crave**.

26. INDOOR PLAY PLACES WERE EVERYWHERE AND SOCIAL GAMING WAS DIFFERENT.

Growing up during the 90s, we saw the rise (and fall) of the "indoor play place". How in the hell *Discovery Zone* **ever** went bankrupt is quite a mystery. That place had slides, ball pits, stuff to climb on *and* indoor mazes. That sounds like a blast in modern times so just imagine how thrilling it must've been for our child selves. Luckily, when *Discovery Zone* filed bankruptcy, they were purchased and turned into an even better place called *Chuck E. Cheese's*! Honestly, is there a combination even close to being as magnificent as pizza, slides, tubes, amusement rides and arcade games? Of course *McDonalds* had their own version of a play place as well that often included the basic pit of balls and slides. Which ever one you preferred, it should be agreed upon that these places were one of the fondest memories of the 1990s.

One of the big draws for *Chuck E. Cheese's* has always been the arcades. People love videogames; always have, always will. Look at the modern social gamer though. They grab their headsets, connect to their wi-fi and battle it out with others down the street and/or across the globe. Is the fact that new video game systems have the ability to do that amazing? Absolutely it is, but the present day social gamer is completely different than we were. We actually went out to arcades and socialized with other kids, facing off with them *in person.*

Arcades during the 90s were like heaven to a kid. Those dimly lit rooms were full of classic games such as:

NBA JAM: Gigantic heads, launching threes, mugging your opponent to get steals, jumping 30 feet in the air to slam dunk, Boomshakalaka!, Bill Clinton and the fear instilled when your challenger went from "heating up" to "on fire". All these things composed the best arcade basketball game ever.

MORTAL KOMBAT II: Blood, guts, gore and more blood. This scared the hell out of our parents who didn't want us to have anything to do with such a violent, graphic game. The fatalities were gruesome but let's be honest - this game had no influence whatsoever on a common sense having kid's mind. We grasped that it was only a game of pixel grisliness and that it was impossible in real life to freeze someone into a block of ice and break 'em to pieces, do flying bicycle kicks, rip their heart out, punch their head off or any of the other vicious acts that went down in MKII. Relax, parents and give us a *little* credit in the smarts department.

MARVEL VS. CAPCOM 2: Holy crap, this game was bananas! Tons of characters from Spider-Man to Mega Man to Ryu to Captain America. Not only was there a massive selection of characters but each person had a very specific move set and their own unique fighting style that created endless possibilities with different combinations of teams.

TEENAGE MUTANT NINJA TURTLES: TURTLES IN TIME: Quite possibly the greatest beat 'em up game ever made, this was as legit as they came. The innovative ability to throw enemies at each other (and even directly into the screen) in addition to a time traveling storyline equaled video game *gold*. One obnoxious common occurrence that we all remember was when you played with a friend and they ate the pizza for health even though they had a full bar while you were on the brink of your demise? That was simply more frustrating than words can describe.

CRAZY TAXI: This game was massively fun for two large reasons; one, we weren't allowed to drive yet so a game that put us behind the wheel earned big props. Secondly, it allowed us to drive around a realistic looking (at the time) city and clumsily crash into everything. Unfortunately missions with quick time constrains filled the game and driving mofos to specific locations within 45 seconds really limited the freedom and amount of havoc one could wreak.

NFL BLITZ: For those who aren't fond of realistic football or its rules, this was the game for them. Let's see, you could lay vicious blows on players, even hitting them after the play was over or you could get away with blatant pass interference and the refs didn't make a peep. Pure brilliance for the fans of unrealistic football! Nothing beats a football game full of fake punt attempts and excessive celebrations.

As cool as it is to play *Madden* from a house in America against an opponent who is in England, the social aspect of gaming it *gone*. In arcades you made friends, enemies, fans and everything in between! Trash talk was rare, and that's because you were **face to face** with your adversary, not behind a headset like the X-box or Playstation online games, which are full of bold speaking, potty mouths. The silly back and forth banter we experienced has evolved into getting called a series of explicit words by a bunch of twelve year olds. If we won, it was usually fairly graciously and if we lost, we expected our conqueror to win with at least a smidgen class.

Ah, the good ol' days. Beat 'em up games, pizza, slides, socializing. We really had the good life, that is for certain. Kids of the nineties decade should appreciate the fact that they actually got to experience *real,* social gaming.

27. WE SPENT COUNTLESS HOURS SEARCHING FOR WALDO & CARMEN SANDIEGO.

At some point during the 90s you undoubtedly spent hours scanning *Where's Waldo* books and watching Carmen Sandiego's cartoon series and/or game show. Waldo and Carmen spent the decade on the run, doing their damndest to stay out of the public eye. The illustrations in *Where's Waldo* books were drawn with the tiniest minutiae being included. Once you found Waldo you could browse through the pages and take a look at the variety of characters and situations taking place around him.

Carmen Sandiego on the other hand had a game show (*Where In The World Is Carmen Sandiego?)* which featured kids trying to solve the woman's location. She also had a cartoon series that portrayed two teens trying to stop the kleptomaniac Sandiego from stealing artifacts around the world. She stole, not for monetary gains but for the challenge and thrills. From time to time she would even drop hints of her location in a taunting fashion, yet searchers were unable to pinpoint her down.

Waldo and Carmen Sandiego were a couple of shifty, sketchy characters – yet we loved chasing after them. It's obvious to see that these two would've made the **perfect** couple. Can you imagine the elusive babies that they would produce?

28. CAPTAIN PLANET'S TEAM HAD A WEAK LINK.

Captain Planet's Planeteers were all extraordinary. Well, all but one…Yeah, we're looking at you, *Ma-Ti*. When the five teenagers from different parts of the globe were summoned by Gaia to defend the world from crime and pollution, each was given a ring. The ability to control an element came along with wearing said ring. What are the four classic elements you ask? Earth, fire, wind and water. If there's a unit being assembled whose sole purpose is to save the planet, those are magnificent element choices to dish out to the team members. But do you know what isn't? Heart. Ma-Ti was the unfortunate Planeteer to possess "heart" which allowed him to instill concern and passion into the people of the world, forcing them to care for the planet.

Honestly Heart would be a pretty cool gift to control if you didn't have to watch four peers receive superior ones right next to you. Think of it this way; what if one day you're at work and your boss decides to bring you and four other employees' gifts. He hands *iPads* to your four co-workers and when he gets to you, he gives you a twenty dollar gift card to *Applebees*. On any other day, had he given you that gift card you would love it! But, because he gave four folks before you something so fantastic, you'd feel jibbed. That's what happened here. Captain Planet gave Kwame, Wheeler, Gi and Linka iPads, leaving Ma-Ti with twenty bucks worth of *Applebees* grub.

The coolest aspect of Ma-Ti's gift was that he could communicate telepathically with animals. Essentially he was a glorified *Dr. Doolittle* who could persuade you to go green. Meanwhile, his fellow Planeteers were capable of starting an earthquake directly under your feet, lighting you on fire, putting you in the eye of an F5 tornado and drowning you. The worst Ma-Ti could do is convince you to pick up trash, recycle cans & bottles, then have a psychic conversation with your dog about it. *Riveting.*

29. DISNEY LOVES TO ADD SUBLIMINAL NAUGHTINESS.

Whether you are a firm believer or a doubter, surely at some point you heard the buzz about multiple subliminal messages Disney placed (or didn't place) in their movies. Some are debatable while others have firm evidence, either way, as nineties kids it's always fun to speculate.

ALADDIN WHISPER-GATE

In *Aladdin*, there's a scene that takes place on Jasmine's balcony in which Aladdin supposedly whispers the phrase, "Good teenagers, take off your clothes." Jasmine's tiger, Rajah is trying to back Aladdin off of the railing so the argument that's often times made is that he's actually saying, "Good kitty, take off and go." It's hard to decide without a shadow of a doubt what is being said but a case can be made that he did, or didn't whisper it. That being said, when it's a close call we really can't give Disney the benefit of the doubt because the likelihood of *all* these innuendo accusations being complete accidents or coincidence is slim.

THE LION KING SEX-GATE

The infamous cloud of dust forming the word "sex" during *The Lion King* is probably the most commonly discussed of these Disney secret message accusations. At one point in the movie, Timon, Pumbaa and Simba are laying down, looking at the stars. Simba goes to the edge of the cliff and plops down, causing some dust to fly in the air. The dirt cloud floats around, swirling into what looks to be a pattern that spells out "sex". It's questionable but it certainly doesn't look far off from the letters s-e-x which is enough evidence for many to believe it's true. Finding this out was pretty fascinating – but not as much as realizing that young Simba is voiced by Jonathon Taylor Thomas, aka Randy Taylor on *Home Improvement*.

THE LITTLE MERMAID PENIS COVER-GATE

Drawn on the cover of *The Little Mermaid* is a castle, which has a piece of its architecture that *strongly* resembles a penis. Many rumors stated that a disgruntled Disney employee on the verge of being fired, angrily drew this phallus as a parting gift, but naysayers argue that the artist who drew the cover didn't actually work for them, which would rule that theory out. The angry employee part may be nonsense but we can't simply chalk it up as an unintentional mistake. Regardless of who drew it and how they felt about Disney, it's safe to say that's a castle penis. However, in the guilty party's defense, the first thing people feel the urge to draw when they want to deface something is typically a penis. It's the universal, go-to move for vandalizing, so perhaps the artist got bored and let immaturity get the best of him.

APPROPRIATE SECRETS HIDDEN IN THE HUNCHBACK OF NOTRE DAME-GATE

If you've been waiting for a hidden piece in a Disney movie that *isn't* sexual or debatable, here you go! In *The Hunchback Of Notre Dame* when Quasimodo sings "Out There" from the rooftop, the camera pans over a street and a few things can be spotted when looking closely. In the right hand corner, is Belle from *Beauty And The Beast*, walking and reading a book in her distinctive blue dress. Also seen is a guy shaking the magic carpet from *Aladdin* and two guys carrying Pumbaa from *Lion King* with a pole.

Nowadays it's a witch hunt and some people will nitpick at any and everything, grasping at straws in attempts to find a subliminal message. While many of the hidden Disney bits from the 90s are debatable, the doubters need keep in mind that mistakes and coincidences do happen, but would they really occur *this* often in the same company's films?

30. WE SPENT A LARGE PORTION OF THE 90s ON A SUGAR HIGH.

As kids during the 1990s whenever we received any type of allowance or extra money, many of us saw this as a good opportunity to satisfy our sweet tooth. The wide selection of candy included chocolates, sweets, sours and everything in between. Let's take a gander at some of the more noteworthy junk foods of our decade.

WARHEADS: Just thinking about 'em can make a person's mouth water. They still exist and it's still extremely challenging to endure the excruciatingly sour taste that comes with them. When it comes to discomfort themed candy, Warheads are among the best.

PIXY STIX: I'm pretty sure this was just colored sugar in a straw that you poured directly into your mouth. It's safe to say that we gained nothing even slightly nutritional from consuming these.

RING POPS/PUSH POPS: Ring Pops were mainly for girls, Push Pops for boys. Ring Pops ("A lollipop without a stick, a ring of flavor you can lick!") were wearable food while Push Pops offered a cap so you could save it for later. It's actually cringe worthy to imagine how disgusting *saving* a used lollipop was, especially since those things seemed to create a gooey, sticky monstrosity when combined with your saliva.

BRACH'S ROCKS: Pebble shaped candy that looked like granite/rock but had a chewy, fruity center. It didn't matter if they tasted good or not, the fact that they resembled rocks but were edible made 'em appealing.

BUTTER FINGER BBs: A form of Butterfingers about the size of a marble, that we devoured by the bag. They were delicious *and* they had Bart Simpson in their commercials! These bad boys emptied many 90s kids Velcro, Ninja Turtles wallets.

SQUEEZE POPS: Quite possibly the worst thing that's ever gone into your body, these things came in the form of red, green or blue oozy, gooeyness. They were supposed to be lollipops in liquid form that could be squeezed from a tube but how disgusting is that concept? Also, if you made the mistake of leaving that cap open, it resulted in one of the stickiest messes ever. Tons of upholstery must've been ruined as a result of Squeeze Pops.

FUN DIP: How's this for unhealthy? Mold a stick made purely out of sugar and dip it into granulated, colored sugar. Pure brilliance.

POP ROCKS: Surrounded by myths and urban legends, many of us ate these and plugged our ears to hear the sizzle in our mouth while others feared that mixing them with soda pop would make your stomach explode like C-4.

JAWBREAKERS: Often times they were too big to be consumed in one outing, forcing us to save these bad boys for another day. That's actually pretty nauseating too, being that we covered 'em in our spit, giving dust, lint and/or germs the perfect place to land.

NERDS: Two flavors. One box. Crunchy. Sweet. Awesome.

VARIOUS FRUIT SNACKS: While they used the word "fruit" loosely and provided very little vitamins or nutrients, fruit snacks were always a big draw for children of the 90s. They came in a variety of forms if you recall there being **Fruit Roll-Ups, Fruit By The Foot, Fruit Gushers** *and* **Shark Bites**.

DUNKAROOS: They weren't "candy" but they're still arguably the single greatest snack in the history of civilization. These kangaroo shaped cookies were flavored cinnamon, honey graham or chocolate chip and came in about 10 cookies per package. Along with the previously mentioned cookies was an ungenerous cubic inch of the most scrumdiddlyumptious icing **ever.** The frosting was flavored chocolate, vanilla or sometimes vanilla with rainbow sprinkles -- perfect for your dipping pleasures. These things do still exist but aren't as easy to find as back in the 90s. Seriously, I'd do far more for some Dunkaroos than I would for a Klondike Bar.

In closing, I'd like to show my appreciation for candy makers of the 1990s. Thanks guys, for the sweet, tasty memories… *And* the cavities… *And* the future diabetes.

31. *HOME ALONE* WOULD'VE BEEN A SHORT FILM IF IT HAD HAPPENED TO US.

Home Alone has become an every year Christmas tradition for many of us, meaning we've watched it plenty of times and evaluated the tiniest of details. We understand that like many movies, *Home Alone* is way beyond the realm of possibilities. If home invasions were this much fun in real life we'd all leave our doors unlocked and put valuables on display in the windows. While we wouldn't necessarily have handled things the same way young Kevin McCallister did, we appreciate his actions because they resulted in two of the best Christmas movies in existence with tons of classic moments such as:

- FOUR WORDS: "I am upstairs, dummy."
- Kevin's parents being on the plane and his mom realizing for the first time that her son has been left at home. Then infamously screaming, "Kevin!"
- Kevin coming face to face with Old Man Marley and running away, screaming.
- Kevin using the sounds from the fictional gangster movie (*Angels With Filthy Souls*) to scare the sh*t out of that poor pizza delivery boy.
- ALL of the booby trap scenes involving Harry and Marv.
- Kevin later becoming friends with Old Man Marley and The Pigeon Lady.
- Old Man Marley reuniting with his daughter.

All these classic moments wouldn't have been possible if Kevin didn't handle things the way he did. That being said, if it was us, this film would've been a lot shorter and far less entertaining. You'd probably see nothing more than a kid calling 911 and waiting patiently for the police to arrive. Thank goodness Macaulay Culkin had so much intestinal fortitude.

32. ANYONE BORN AFTER THE 90s WON'T APPRECIATE TECHNOLOGY.

Growing up during the 90s, we are the last generation to experience a portion of our lives without certain technologies – specifically computers and the internet. Now that kids have Facebook by age twelve and a massive serving of X-box Live/Playstation Network to go along with it, they'll be too consumed by modern day technology to ever experience, or truly appreciate *many* things.

TECHNOLOGY DURING THE 90s

1) VCRs & VHS TAPES: If you're new enough in the world to only be familiar with DVDs and Blu-rays then consider yourself lucky. Being able to rewind, fast forward and select scenes *so quickly* is a luxury to those of us who once had to struggle with finding a precise part of a movie on VHS. Not to mention the hi-definition picture that DVD and Blu-ray users have been blessed with. It's odd because VCRs were such a pain in the rear, but in a strange way, we miss 'em… Or at least the times that came along with them.

2) CASSETTE & CD PLAYERS: When tapes were the dominant form of listening to music, a lot of the same issues we had with VHS tapes occurred. We all remember waiting by the radio to press record and stop when we made mix-tapes. Or having to rewind and fast forward until we found our desired song. Then, when CD players came out they provided us with the ability to skip songs by the press of a button. Really, that was pretty impressive until *Apple iPods* came along with their ability to hold more songs than you could possibly want (or know), while also being capable of playing games, videos *and* going online.

3) PHONES: Cellular wasn't really popular until the latter part of the decade and even then they were the size of bricks, and we (as kids) didn't have one. What we had was a house phone. A house phone that **didn't** send text messages, play our favorite tunes when it rang and more importantly, didn't offer us a clue as to who was calling. Before 'Caller ID' existed, you answered your phone at your own risk, without the slightest idea who was on the other end.

4) DIAL-UP INTERNET: If you had internet before all the DSL or high speed business, you know what Dial-Up was all about. For a good 30 seconds we heard a combination of dialing, beeps, boops and screeches as our computers connected ever so slowly to the internet. Even once we were online, pages loaded *sooo slooowly*. So in modern time, if your computer ever freezes for a few seconds or the internet isn't working at the speed of light, *relax*. Because there once was a time when the internet worked at the pace of the DMV.

If you're young enough to have never rewound a movie after watching it, used a phone that had a cord, or been kicked off of the internet so your parents could use their **corded, caller-id less** phone, you're certainly *not* a 90s kid.

*"We grew up playing outside with no Internet or *Facebook*" is the 90s kid's version of our grandparents' "We had to walk 5 miles in the snow barefoot, back and forth!" stories.

33. YOU HAD TO BE ON DRUGS TO RIDE THE MAGIC SCHOOL BUS.

Plenty of us had perfect attendance based solely on the fact that we held out hope that one day, our bus rides would somehow turn magical. *The Magic School Bus'* books and cartoon series made 90s kids want to ride that splendidly supernatural, yellow transporter to space, the rainforest, back in time or wherever it was headed on any given day!

Upon reflection, it's evident that there's more than meets the eye when it comes to Miss Frizzle. No, I'm not saying she's a transformer, but surely there was something influencing her wacky ways and allowing her to go on such amazing adventures. What could it be? My best guess is some form(s) of narcotics. Was Miss Frizzle really taking those kids on journeys to incredible locations or was she simply tripping on acid? And more importantly, was she distributing those same remedies to her students, allowing them to see the same things as her and follow along on those voyages? These are the questions that should've been asked back in '95!

side note: There was also a Magic School Bus computer game for kids that was the LEGIT.

34. REN, STIMPY AND ROCKO ARE STILL ENTERTAINING, FOR NEW REASONS.

One of the commonalities many cartoons from the 1990s share is the adult jokes and innuendo, laced throughout many episodes. Some did it more commonly than others and while we didn't notice it *then*, watching these series' now often results in 90s kids being taken aback by some of the ridiculousness cartoon makers got away with. Often we were amused by the physical comedy or the potty humor, failing to understand 100% of what we were seeing. Want to be rattled by some of the content that was a part of your childhood? Read on.

REN & STIMPY

- Hefty servings of violence **and** fart/booger jokes.
- Grossness including but not limited to: bulging veins, butt cheeks, pimples and lumpy, disgusting images that weren't ideal for a children's series.
- Not educational in anyway whatsoever which drew heat from parents.
- A scene in which Ren plucks nerve endings from his gums.
- A scene where Ren beats the living sh*t out of a guy with a boat oar.
- Homosexual innuendo. Lots of it.

ROCKO'S MODERN LIFE

- Pushed the envelope, often times resulting in scenes being changed or cut by the network.
- The main characters' favorite place to eat was a diner called "The Chokey Chicken".
- In one episode, Rocko gets hired as a phone-sex operator. Rocko is seen on the phone saying "Oh baby, oh baby, oh baby" in an unenthused, monotone manner to the other person on the line who turns out to be another character, Mrs. Bighead. Also, a sign in Rocko's cubicle read: "Be hot, be naughty, be courteous."

- There was a scene where Rocko is picking berries from a bush and inadvertently grabs a bear's genitals.
- During a hospital scene a call is head for "Doctor Philiac, Doctor NecroPhiliac".
- A scene in which Rocko and company are watching a horror film titled: "Night of the Shaved Kittens". (If you don't understand this innuendo *now*, you probably never will.)

While many may find these things appalling, others do enjoy the fact that they can appreciate cartoons from over a decade ago, for a whole new set of reasons. Whatever your stance is, the fact remains that there were some perverted, violent, sick, twisted minds working over at *Nickelodeon*.

35. *TEENAGE MUTANT NINJA TURTLES* RULED ON SO MANY LEVELS.

Teenage Mutant Ninja Turtles is worthy of a decade achievement award in the eyes of a good chunk of 90s kids. Why? Well, it was an extremely successful franchise that existed in just about every possible form.

THE CARTOON: They never really used their weapons, yet they totally kicked ass. The four heroes in half shells fought off the likes of ~~Uncle Phil,~~ Shredder, Bebop, Rocksteady and Krang much to our entertainment.

THE COMICS: A more violent version of the cartoon on pages, it was excellent from the stories to the illustrations.

ACTION FIGURES: Boatloads of Ninja Turtles toys existed in a variety of formats. There were themes such as Mutant Militant, Wacky Wild West and Sewer Sports All-Stars to name a few.

MOVIES: Three films during the 90s (*Teenage Mutant Ninja Turtles, Teenage Mutant Ninja Turtles II: The Secret of the Ooze* & *Teenage Mutant Ninja Turtles III*) that made lots of moolah and, with the exception of part III, were well reviewed. The movies managed to stay loyal to the comics while incorporating aspects from the cartoon and delivering the goods to Ninja Turtles fans across the globe.

ICE CREAM BARS: Delicious ice cream/sherbet bars. Bubblegum eyes. Epic, deliciousness.

VIDEO GAME: Multiple games including *Teenage Mutant Ninja Turtles: Turtles In Time.* Up to four players (two for Super Nintendo users) opening up a can of whoop ass on the "Foot Soldiers" never got old. Not to mention the game had the Ninja Turtles in a time warp and featured cowboy ninjas, cavemen creatures, and other monsters among the long list of enemies. An action packed arcade game that managed to maintain the essence of the Ninja Turtles we all knew and loved.

36. WE ALL WANTED TO ATTEND *TINY TOON ADVENTURES'* ACME LOONIVERSITY.

The place where one earns their "toon degree" seemed quite appealing as a child. Acme Looniversity is the name of the school that the characters from *Tiny Toon Adventures* graced with their presence. It was a pretty star studded school, the list of professors included:

Bugs Bunny, Elmer Fudd, Sylvester Cat, Daffy Duck, Foghorn Leghorn, Taz, Wile E. Coyote, Pepé Le Pew Yosemite Sam, Road Runner, Porky Pig, Tweety Bird and Speedy Gonzalez.

The students often resembled their elder instructors but didn't necessarily act like them. **Babs** and **Buster Bunny** were partners in crime who had a crush on each other. Besides being pink, Babs was steadily hyper and willing to do anything for a laugh while Buster was the calmer, bluer leader of the Tiny Toons. **Plucky Duck** was the son of Daffy and quite the egomaniac, often taking part in various shenanigans for individual glory or personal satisfaction. Plucky was BFFs with **Hampton J. Pig**, the most easy going character of 'em all. Hampton was a neat freak who on very rare occasions, snapped when his patience was tested a little *too much*.

Dizzy was a young Tasmanian Devil who wasn't quite the brightest crayon in the box. The guy wore a beanie with a propeller on it, had two different colored eyes, constantly drooled (spitting when he spoke), ate damn near anything and moved around by spinning in a destructive tornado form. Then there was young **Elmyra Duff** who was borderline psychotic, obsessing over animals and all things cute. Typically she'd cause great discomfort or injuries to creatures with overenthusiastic affection that included squeezing the living sh*t out of 'em. Elmyra's unfortunate, unwilling pet was **Furrball**, but he wasn't the only person getting her attention. The rich, spoiled brat (every school has one), **Montana Max** was often on the receiving end of Elmyra's fondness. He lived in a huge mansion, had a short temper and a whopping total of *zero* friends besides Elmyra.

Tiny Toon Adventures was and still is loved by many 90s kids who enjoyed seeing all the foolishness that went down in the fictional town of Acme Acres. Ahh, explosives, anvils dropped on heads and all other forms of slapstick -- cartoon humor never gets old.

OTHER CHARACTERS ON *TINY TOON ADVENTURES*:

Sweetie Pie, Little Beeper, Lil' Sneezer, Calamity Coyote, Fifi La Fume, Shirley the Loon, Gogo Dodo, Concord Condor, Fowlmouth, Bookworm, Barky Marky, Banjo Possum, Mary Melody.

37. WE CARRY THE BOY BAND BURDERN.

Like most people, 90s kids aren't exactly thrilled with every aspect of our past. One thing that we have the misfortune of being responsible for is the success of those cheese-tastic boy bands. The poppy, obnoxious, overplayed, overpaid groups were seemingly *everywhere*. Our decade's last few years were hit with a bombardment of different pop sensation groups and many of us purchased the albums and merchandise, funding the production of more and more of their jingles. Let's reflect on each group and what tunes they are responsible for embedding in our brains.

HANSON: Mmmbop, ba dubi dop, ba du bop, ba dubi dop, ba du bop, ba dubi dop, ba du... Yeah, Yeah!... That will now be stuck in your head for the next 7-10 hours. Enjoy.

BACKSTREET BOYS: The best selling boy band in history with over 130 *million* records sold world wide. "*I'll Never Break Your Heart*", "*Quit Playing Games (With My Heart)*" and "*I Want It That Way*" were among the loooong list of hits released by this group. Their fans and radio stations alike were quite dedicated to playing their songs on rapid repeat, over and over until our ears bled.

***NSYNC:** JC, Justin, Lance, Joey and Chris formed the band *NSYNC and dispensed hits like "Tearin' Up My Heart", "I Want You Back", "Bye Bye Bye" and (too) many more. They split up in the early 2000s but you hear about 'em in the news as individuals occasionally. I mean, Justin Timberlake is all over the place doing romantic comedies and showcasing his acting abilities while Lance Bass has a show on *Sirius Satellite Radio*. JC Chasez produces, writes and sings in addition to being a host on *America's Best Dance Crew* on MTV. Meanwhile Joey Fatone is narrating *Family Feud* and Chris Kirkpatrick is... well... um, I think he's alive - at least, his *Wikipedia* **doesn't** say he's dead, so we'll assume he's still

somewhere, breathing.

98 DEGREES: They saw the *Backstreet Boys* and **NSYNC's* success and said, "Hell, we can do that too!" Four vocalists. Nick Lachey is probably the only member you can still name. "Because Of You" and "The Hardest Thing" were their breakthrough hits. Their album *98 Degrees and Rising* went 4x platinum so some of you likely bought (and possibly still own) them. Don't be ashamed; embrace your admiration of clichéd love songs.

*Hair care product makers surely made a fortune off of the high demand of dye kits sought after by the foolish fans who wanted to rock the freshly frosted tips look of their boy band idols.

38. FULL HOUSE'S DANNY TANNER & JOEY GLADSTONE ARE NOT WHO WE THOUGHT THEY WERE.

By "Full House", they meant house full of lies and frauds. Watching *Full House* as a kid, we became so familiar with the shows characters that we almost felt as if we *knew* them. Turns out, we didn't. Bob Saget, who played Danny Tanner is arguably the greatest actor of his generation once we realized how far off he was from his character in real life.

WHAT YOU *THOUGHT* IN 1993: Danny Tanner is a great father. The poor man lost his wife to a drunk driver car accident, has three daughters and does a damn good job of raising them solo. He's ridiculously kind, understanding and overall a gentle, well spoken man. Also, he likes to clean things. A lot. Oh, and there's no way he ever cusses, **ever.**

WHAT YOU *KNOW* NOW: Oh Mylanta, Bob Saget cusses?! He's the polar opposite of Danny Tanner. Saget is a funny yet extremely vulgar comedian and actor who has taken on roles that would've shocked our prepubescent selves. From a former drug addict in *Half Baked* to a hooker loving version of himself on *Entourage*. Then he has his stand-ups which consist of sailor-esque amounts of explicit words. It's genuinely hard to watch Bob Saget out of the Danny Tanner role for your first time! Trust me, seeing him declare, "I used to suck d*** for coke!" in the movie *Half Baked* was a traumatizing experience that ripped an irreparable hole in the fabric of my childhood.

Now let's move on to Dave Coulier, aka Joey Gladstone. The guy had all the *ingredients that make up a creepy "uncle". While we thought he was kind of a bum who, on the show had an unsteady job (failing comedian), a bad haircut and mooched off of Danny Tanner and company, we were dead wrong. You wanna know what Joey Gladstone was doing during the 90s? Alanis Morissette, that's what -- or shall I say, "who". Alanis was one of the biggest female musicians of the decade and Dave Coulier must've had some type of smooth jive talk to tingle Morissette's loins.

Whatever the case, their relationship soured at some point. Many speculate that Coulier wanted to start a family and Alanis (15 years his junior) felt too young and rejected that concept. Dave, the smooth mofo that he was, found a new lady friend and got over Morissette too quickly for her liking. Thus, the song "*You Oughta Know*" came into this world and totally revolved around Dave Coulier. Here's an example of the lyrics directed at him:

Did you forget about me?
Mr. Duplicity, I hate to bug you in the middle of dinner.
It was a slap in the face, how quickly I was replaced.
*Are you thinking of me when you fu*k her?*

Pretty extreme, right? There's even a part in the song where she mentions performing an oral sex act on her ex-lover in a movie theatre. Now, Alanis has all but confirmed that it's about Coulier but it has to be true, I mean, it's all over the internet[1]. The overall coolness of the story automatically boosts Joey Gladstone and Dave Coulier's stock. Let's not get out of hand here though; John Stamos is the coolest dude on that show, bar none. To this day, Uncle Jesse is *still* the man.

*THE JOEY GLADSTONE CREEPY "UNCLE" RECIPE

3 cups of Cut.It.Out.
2 tbsp Popeye Impressions.
1 woodchuck ventriloquist act.
1/3 cup of various annoying cartoon impressions.

Add ingredients into an ugly Hawaiian shirt or hockey jersey, stir and serve chilled and unfunny. For extra creepiness, live in the basement, fully invest yourself in three little girls lives and show minimal interest in dating women your age.

[1]I hope you knew I was kidding about the internet's reliability. Good Lord, the world needs a sarcasm font desperately.

39. POKÈMON WAS A PRETTY CRUEL CONCEPT.

Gotta Catch 'Em All' was the motto that these ruthless Pokémon trainers lived by, and for a long time we thought what they were doing was all fun and games. Ash Ketchum and his crew (Misty & Brock) trotted the globe in pursuit of one common goal: being the world's best Pokémon breeder. Unfortunately, the notion that it's acceptable to hunt and capture these creatures, then force them to fight for your own personal gain is pretty messed up, for many reasons.

First of all, it indirectly and probably unintentionally makes things like dog or cockfighting seem somewhat acceptable. I'm not saying that Michael Vick could've pled "not guilty" and blamed his actions on *Pokémon*, but it *could* potentially have some influence on the mindset of youths.

4 REASONS WHY POKÈMON FIGHTING IS CRUEL.

1. Pokémon are living creatures with a decent amount of intelligence.
2. To catch a Pokémon, you send another Pokémon to whip it's ass until it's weak enough to capture.
3. After beating a Pokémon senseless, the trainer zaps it into an undersized 'Pokéball', where is spends its spare time. They don't look particularly spacious *or* comfy.
4. The only time that a Pokémon gets out of said Pokéball is when they are needed to come to blows with another Pokémon in battle.

Can you imagine how blazing, hot Charmander or any other fire natured Pokémon was inside that itty, bitty Pokéball? Or how much it would suck to have to fight your own kind? Regardless of it's implications and similarities to animal cruelty, it's a highly successful global phenomenon that many of us enjoyed.

POKÈMON FUN FACTS

- Pokémon #23, Ekans is Snake spelled backwards. His evolved version, #24, Arbok is Kobra in reverse. (Even though, "cobra" is the proper spelling.)
- The original Ash Ketchum voice was done by a woman (Veronica Taylor).
- When Pokémon #60, Poliwag evolves into #61 Poliwhirl, the swirl on its stomach changes directions.
- Jessie and James of Team Rocket are 17 years old.
- When a Pikachu meets another Pikachu, they don't shake hands, they greet by interlocking tails.

40. SOME OF OUR CHILDHOOD MOVIES ARE SO BAD THAT THEY'RE CLASSICS.

When we were kids we tended to be a lot less critical of films and a lot easier to entertain and amuse. But now as we age and grow smarter, those opinions change – sometimes drastically. Everyone has had those WTF-WIT[1] moments where they watch a movie that was considered a classic growing up, but now it's cringe worthy and every minute viewed is a crushing blow to your adolescent self's world. It's time to evaluate the movies that are shamefully buried somewhere deep in our basements on VHS tapes.

KAZAAM:

Short Synopsis: Shaquille O'Neal plays a rapper/genie. That alone should've indicated the disaster of a movie that was to come.
Rating as a kid (1-10): 6 – Only because the kid wished for all that candy and seeing boatloads of M&Ms and chocolate bars was a fantasy. You gotta remember, as kids, junk food was as enjoyable as of attractive members of the opposite sex. So when *Kazaam* showed us a warehouse full of sweets, it was the equivalent of seeing your favorite Hollywood star in a shirtless/topless scene.
Rating now (1-10): 2 – It's still unintentionally hilarious.
Best Part Of The Film: The end credits.
Worst Part Of The Film: Everything else.
Final Thoughts: This movie confirms that shooting free throws isn't the only thing Shaq is terrible at. Legend has it that if you smear poop on the inside of a VCR, *Kazaam* automatically starts playing.

SUPER MARIO BROTHERS

Short Synopsis: A live action version of a beloved video game series in which The Mario Brothers attempt to save Princess Daisy.
Rating as a kid (1-10): 8.5 – It was highly inaccurate but still very cool to see the characters that we'd controlled in a game, on the big screen.
Rating now (1-10): 6 – It remains a decently entertaining movie to

this day. For those that hate it, you have to realize that it was a transition *from video game to film*. Changes were mandatory. How ridiculous would it have looked if they had Mario hitting bricks with his head, eating mushrooms, growing larger, jumping on Goomba heads and shooting fireballs? It would've been preposterous. This was an adaptation, folks! Take it for what it's worth and enjoy its ridiculousness.

Best Part Of The Film: Bob Hoskins and John Leguizamo being over the top and awesome as Mario and Luigi.

Worst Part Of The Film: That it's associated with Mario. If you take away the fact that it's supposed to be a Mario based movie, people probably would've enjoyed it. Good actors, decent special effects and a solid story -- it seems the only thing that causes this movie to draw so much heat is the video game aspects it's lacking.

Final Thoughts: As likable as Hoskins and Leguizamo are, they simply aren't the best casting choices for the **MARIO BROTHERS**. Mainly because Mario and Luigi are supposed to be ***Italians*** with ***mustaches***. Hoskins is an Englishman and Leguizamo is a clean shaven, Puerto Rican.

BATMAN & ROBIN

Short Synopsis: It was supposed to be a film based **on the iconic *Batman* franchise**. I'm not quite sure the creators ever got that memo because they created a very ludicrous two hour shit show.

Rating as a kid (1-10): 7 - We saw Batman in his bat suit so automatically this film got cool points and was considered watchable by our younger selves. Plus, Poison Ivy (Uma Thurman) was appealing and there were action sequences which was good enough for us at the time.

Rating now (1-10): .5 - It's awful. So awful that it's hard to look away. You might think that having big stars like Clooney and Schwarzenegger would result in a decent film but that is not the case. It's worthy of just about as low a rating as one can possibly give.

Best Part Of The Film: Whenever Arnold Schwarzenegger (Mr. Freeze) uses the words "chill", "freeze", "cool" and/or "cold" as a God awful pun. I mean, even though ***icy*** what he was doing, it's still hilarious.

Worst Part Of The Film: Unfortunately there isn't a sufficient amount of paper in the world to print out the worst parts of *Batman & Robin* on.

Final Thoughts: This movie is the drunken, ugly mistake that never should've happened. It is the disappointment you feel when you think you found a parking spot but a small car or motorcycle is already there. It is the opposite of good but far worse than bad.

HONORABLE MENTION

BABY GENIUSES: This movie (and it's sequel) have a comfy spot in the Internet Movie Database's bottom 100 films for good reason.
MORTAL KOMBAT: It's kind of sad, but as subpar as this movie was, you can make a case that this is the best video game adaptation film (besides *Prince of Persia: The Sands of Time.*)
BIO-DOME: The leading man is Pauly Shore so, yeah... Once you make that casting decision you've decided to set the bar of expectations low.

On the bright side, if you're still interested in owning any of these movies, you can probably find 'em in Wal-Mart's bin of crappy DVDs for a buck or two.

1. WTF-WIT = What the f*ck was I thinking?

41. EVERY *ANIMANIACS* SEGMENT WAS WORTH OF A SPIN-OFF.

When you hear '*Animaniacs*', it's likely that Yakko, Wakko and Dot come to mind first. It's only right that they do since they were the stars and carried the load for the humor heavy series. Whether they were being chased through the *Warner Brothers* lot, going gaga over the well endowed *Hello Nurse* or participating in some other type of monkeyshines & mischief, they were consistently hilarious. The series had adult material and innuendo plastered throughout various episodes, making it a perfect candidate to re-watch as an adult. The show gained plenty of fans, for good reason – it offered a diverse selection of other segments that varied in length and content, giving it somewhat of a sketch comedy feel. Recall the other magnificent toons that starred on Animaniacs below.

PINKY AND THE BRAIN: Smart mouse + imbecile mouse = ~~Animated, rodent version of Kenan & Kel?~~ The Pinky and The Brain. When the highly intelligent *Brain* concocted some type of mastermind plan to take over the world, he had *Pinky*'s stupidity to negate any progress made. It was so awesome that it had it's own successful spinoff series.

SLAPPY SQUIRREL: A female squirrel who liked to use explosives and smack the hell out of people, fittingly named *Slappy*. She had a nephew named *Skippy* who was consistently upbeat and chipper. Skippy idolized his famous Aunt Slappy, despite the fact that they were polar opposites. Upon reflection, this aging, abrasive squirrel who liked to hit folks with her purse was pretty awesome.

THE GOODFEATHERS: Revolved around the most gangsta pigeons ever, bar none! *Bobby*, *Squit*, and *Pesto* were spoofs of the characters played by Joe Pesci, Ray Liotta and Robert De Niro in the movie *Goodfellas*. They argued, fussed, bickered and fought – many times resulting in Pesto beating the mess out of Squit. The physical comedy alone was enough to entertain us as kids but this series aged well, remaining very watchable to this day.

RITA AND RUNT: A rather unintelligent dog (*Runt*) and a singing cat (*Rita*) traveled the globe in search of a place to call home. Of course it never went smoothly and plenty of hijinks ensued.

MINERVA MINK: Of the entire ensemble cast, *Minerva* was featured in the fewest segments, quite possibly because of the overt sexuality involved in her pieces (by "her pieces", I mean the sketches revolving around Minerva). She drove the fellas crazy, turning them into babbling, lustful goons. Minerva becomes somewhat promiscuous herself when she saw an attractive guy adopting a, dare I say, slutty attitude. If we were into animated minks, she would be the belle of the ball.
BUTTONS AND MINDY: I think we can all agree that *Mindy* and her Mother deserved a great big "F YOU!" That little girl was constantly breaking out of her harness and her Mom (who was a crappy enough parent to have been on *Rugrats)* was never around to take care of her own kid. *Buttons* being the good hearted dog that he was, went through heaps of trouble to save Mindy's unsupervised self. And what did Buttons get in return? A belly rub? No. A new squeaky toy? Nope. Some *Beggin' Strips*? Absolutely not! Not even a "thank you" was issued to Buttons. Instead, Mindy's ungrateful Mom undeservingly scolded and punished him. As kids we wanted so badly to jump into our television in animated form and punch Mindy's Mother in her face that was never shown (only her legs were ever visible).
GOOD IDEA/BAD IDEA: *Mr. Skullhead* who never spoke a single word was used in these segments, narrated by Tom Bodett. It would first show what was described as a "Good Idea", which depicted Mr. Skullhead involved in some type of normal, pleasant activity. Then, the narrator explained a "Bad Idea" which was a similar task, with a minor yet crucial detail changed. All these years later, it's still capable of delivering a chuckle.
EXAMPLE:
Good Idea: Buying a pair of shoes on sale. Bad Idea: Buying a parachute on sale.

Other characters/sketches that are *Google-Worthy:*
- Baynarts "Charlton" Woodchucks.
- Chicken Boo
- Mr. Director
- Flavio and Marita
- The Mime

42. DISNEY'S ONE SATURDAY MORNING & DISNEY AFTERNOONS WERE PURE BRILLIANCE.

It's actually quite sad to reflect on these respective two hour blocks of kid's television, because they truly hold a special place in our hearts. Saturday mornings were *everything* to 90s kids. For *Disney's One Saturday* Morning, we woke early, poured an oversized bowl of our favorite sugary cereal, plopped on the couch and simply indulged ourselves in a massive helping of childhood – something the youth nowadays don't seem to get a taste of. Even when Saturday mornings were over, we still had plenty of opportunities to watch cartoons and one of those occasions was provided by *The Disney Afternoons*. Let's take some time to remember some of the popular series' that were in each block at one time or another.

DISNEY'S ONE SATURDAY MORNING:

RECESS: T.J. Detweiler led his posse (Spinelli, Vince, Gus, Gretchen and Mikey) around the 'Third Street School" campus like a mother-funking boss. It was farfetched at times but still managed to capture the general feel of elementary school.

PEPPER ANN: The story of a 12 year old ginger in middle school is going to have its ups and downs, which Pepper Ann definitely did. It was somewhat of a girls cartoon, with several strong willed female characters who didn't exactly embrace femininity.

DISNEY'S DOUG: Many of us disliked plenty of things about this revamped version[1] but ultimately, most of us tuned in. Why? Well we probably just wanted our Doug fix, even if he wore those stupid long sleeves and full length khaki pants, instead of the original shorts.

101 DALMATIONS: You know the general concept: bunch of dogs + Cruella de Vil = plenty of predictable but entertaining episodes.

HERCULES: THE ANIMATED SERIES: A spin-off of the 1997 film of the same title. It was teenage Hercules dealing with lots of adolescent nonsense and it contradicted the original movie quite often.

MICKEY MOUSE WORKS: A variety of cartoons with a variety of characters including Mickey, Minnie, Donald & Daisy Duck, Goofy, Pluto and more. It featured several skits that were different lengths, much like *Animaniacs* and *Tiny Toon Adventures* did. Tickled the fancies of 90s kids around the world.

THE DISNEY AFTERNOON:

DUCKTALES: *Ducktales* (a-woo-hoo) had one of, if not the greatest cartoon opening theme songs of all time! Besides that, it was a great children's series and watching that greedy bastard *Scrooge McDuck* regularly try to increase his already massive funds while raising his awesome nephews, Huey, Dewey and Louie was a damn good time back in the day. Scrooge had a vault full of gold and wads of cash that several villains (The Beagle Boys, Flintheart Glomgold and Magica De Spell) were constantly attempting to steal. This show is the reason one of your goals in life is to swim in a mountain of gold.

TALESPIN: Many of the show's characters were inspired by characters from *The Jungle Book. TaleSpin* was one of the better written animated series' of it's decade. *Baloo* and his orphan sidekick, *Kit Cloudkicker* went on entertaining adventures that made us all consider being a pilot. The all work, no play Rebecca Cunningham was constantly up Baloo's ass because of his laidback (borderline lazy) work ethic. Rebecca's daughter *Molly* was a thrill seeking six year old who often tagged along with Kit & Ballo, providing plenty of humor. The only odd part of this cartoon was the fact that Baloo wore a shirt but no pants, leaving his bare, bear ass on full display. Seriously, bro - you're a pilot, surely you can afford a pair of khakis or *something.*

DARKWING DUCK: If *Batman* was an anthropomorphic duck, this would be the result. This was largely responsible for 90s kids' love of after school cartoons. Drake Mallard was a mild-mannered, single parent - but his alter ego, Darkwing Duck was an action providing hero who often found himself in slapstick humor filled battles with criminals and villains. The toon was a parody of the popular superheroes (e.g. *Batman, Green Hornet, The Shadow, Doc Savage,* etc.) and Darkwing himself is a satirical character. Regardless of it's nature, *Darkwing Duck* is definitely worthy of having a modern day video game or movie made about it.

CHIP 'N DALE RESCUE RANGERS: Here's the premise: Two chipmunks who have a knack for finding trouble open up their own detective agency. Hmm, for any kid that sounds rather enticing. *Chip* looked like *Indiana Jones* while *Dale* resembled *Thomas Magnum* (*Magnum P.I.*).The tiny duo handled crimes that the humans didn't, often running into arch enemies, *Fat Cat* (the mobster/mafia looking, overweight feline) and Norton Nimnul (the crazy scientist). Great stories, writing and characters resulted in this often underrated, overlooked cartoon.

GOOF TROOP: *Goofy* and his son *Max* living life in the town of Spoonerville was one of our favorite things to watch. This fantastic cartoon resulted in *A Goofy Movie* which holds a special place in the heart of 99% of 90s kids. The fact that Max was normal and Goofy was so... goofy, provided a good chunk of the comedy.

GARGOYLES: Holy moly, what an epic/badass cartoon this was! It's arguably the darkest, most complex animated series of the decade. The nocturnal Gargoyles were stone during the day but active at night. The six stone creatures were from the year 994 so they spent their time adjusting to modern New York and avoiding various supernatural threats, not only for their safety, but that of the entire world. For those who didn't get their Gargoyles fix from the show's three seasons (78 total episodes) a comic series *and* Sega Genesis video game were created for your viewing and playing pleasures.

BONKERS: Have you seen *Who Framed Roger Rabbit?* Well, this cartoon was a glass full of *Who Framed Roger Rabbit?* Unfortunately, someone put too much ice in the drink and a watered down for kids version was the result.

ALADDIN: It was basically the Disney movie that we knew and loved in half hour increments. It picked up where the movie left off, with Aladdin living in his giant palace along side his lovely Princess Jasmine. It was a good series but it's rather depressing to think about, considering how far modern toons have fallen.

[1]10 THINGS THAT DISNEY'S DOUG CHANGED FROM THE ORIGINAL.

1. The new whistling theme was bleh. Original theme (Doo-doo-do-do-do-do-do-do-do-doodoo) fo' life.
2. Original Doug: Eight strands of hair. Disney's Doug: Nine.
3. Disney's Doug added a younger sister to the Funnie family. Her name was Cleopatra and she served no purpose.
4. Patti got a new haircut and a tan. The updated look enhanced her boyish charm to a level that made Doug go more Gaga than Lady over Ms. Mayonnaise.
5. Roger Klotz became rich. He lives in trailer park for three seasons on Nickelodeon and suddenly the series' biggest douche was rollin' in the dough? Not what the fans want to see.
6. The lightning bolt on Skeeter's shirt was changed to the number **zero**... Possibly to represent the total amount of positive alterations they were making?
7. Nickelodeon's Doug episodes were split into two 11 minute segments. Disney's was one, full 22 minute piece.
8. The Honker Burger (where Doug and friends hung out on the original series) closed down.
9. Connie Benge lost like 50 pounds and was now skinny on Disney's Doug.
10. Disney's Doug BROKE UP THE GREATEST FICTION BAND OF ALL TIME, THE BEETS. That was easily the most angering transformation of them all.

43. *SAVED BY THE BELL* WAS NOTHING LIKE HIGH SCHOOL OR REAL LIFE IN GENERAL.

Perhaps it's our own faults for entrusting in a sitcom to be the trailer/preview to the movie of our future high school experiences, but many of us did and lo and behold -- it was absolutely *nothing* like the folks at Bayside High School portrayed it to be. Sadly, we learned that it was a lot more jocks, jerks, drama, douches, tools, traitors, sluts, brats, rich kids, poor kids, crazies, fatties, geeks, love, heartbreak, lust, hate, snitching, gossip, rumors, rude teachers, *ruder* administrators, rules, restrictions and homework – and a lot less of **everything** we saw on *Saved By The Bell.* Let's evaluate some of the other aspects that never came to fruition, besides the whole *Zack Morris-breaking-the-fourth-wall-talking-directly-into-the-cameras-thing*.

Nerds didn't hang with the cool crowd. On SBTB, Screech walked, talked, dressed and did everything else in stereotypical nerd fashion yet he was in a clique with a popular guy, a jock, a cheerleader and a rich girl. Let's be honest, this simply doesn't happen in real life because glasses, proper English, a disinterest in fashion and a desire to learn are frowned upon by young adults who want to fit in with the popular bunch.

Attractive people aren't typically intelligent AND friendly. We've met attractive and intelligent people. We've met attractive and friendly people. On the rarest of rare occasions, we've met someone who possesses beauty, brains & friendliness. The issue here was that those types of people are such a rare breed that the chances of finding **five** attractive, intelligent, friendly people in one group of friends like Zack, AC, Lisa, Kelly and Jessie, is slim to none. The likelihood of them embracing Screech's dorky ass into their circle are even slimmer.

High school relationships don't always survive. In fact, high school relationships are living on borrowed time the instant they begin. See, the "flavor of the month" type flings that occur during those four precious years of school aren't the least bit serious. Sure, once in a while you'll find a legitimate couple who moves forward dating into college, and sometimes even ends up married -- but the majority of them aren't. So, as great as it is to watch friendships like the Saved By The Bell gang's on TV, real life consists of far more breakups and backstabbing that ultimately ends relationships of platonic or romantic nature. Bottom line, Zack and Kelly were fantastic together, but for most of us – it just didn't go down that perfectly.

44. MCGWIRE & SOSA SAVED MAJOR LEAGUE BASEBALL.

Besides "Simpson", these are the most famous "Homers" of the 1990s. It was the summer of '98 and along came one of the greatest record breaking races in the history of sports. Not only was the battle of homeruns between Sammy Sosa and Mark McGwire a storyline of epic proportions – it also saved all of Major League Baseball's rear ends.

A few years earlier in 1994-1995 baseball had a 232 day strike that led to the cancelation of the '94 World Series. When baseball finally returned, fans were a combination of angry, disappointed and sad with the way things played out, resulting in a massive decline in attendance and ratings. Essentially, the amount of people paying money to go to games and turning baseball on their television was plummeting and they were headed straight into a dark tunnel.
Then, a few years later, a ray of light appeared in the form of two large men. Sammy Sosa of the Chicago Cubs and Mark McGwire of the St. Louis Cardinals burst on the scene jacking homerun after homerun and eventually, people realized they were within range of breaking the previous record for most homers in a season (61).

In Hollywood movie fashion, the two went back and forth in the race. One day McGwire would hit a long ball, and then Sosa would do the same the next day to match it. The chase for history came to a thrilling conclusion when, in a game against each other McGwire finally hit number 62 (his shortest homer of the season that barely made it over the wall), shattering the record books in dramatic fashion. This race ended up reeling so many ex-fans back in *and* drawing masses of new ones that it put baseball back on the map. Cool story, right? Well, not so much anymore. It wasn't until the mid-late 2000s that we found out our slugging, baseball saving 90s heroes were actually juiced up on 'roids. So while they did save baseball, their performance enhanced, historic contest will forever be tainted.

45. OUR LINGO WAS DA BOMB.

The vernacular used during the 90s teeters on the fine line between ridiculous and genius. It's only right that we all take a gander at some of the gibberish we spoke (and sometimes still speak), in our lovely decade.

All that (and a bag of chips). A phrase generally used to describe people who perceived themselves to be the best ("and a bag of chips" = the best *and then some*).
As if! It was the equivalent of saying, "Yeah, right!" We can thank *Clueless* and Alicia Silverstone for this nugget of brilliance.
The (da) bomb! Basically it meant excellence. It's survived the 2000s and people still use it in a different form, describe good things as being "bomb". e.g. "That Taco Bell was bomb!"
Boo Ya! A phrase of exclamation after you've done something noteworthy.
Bounce. To leave.
Chillin'. Just hanging out, relaxing.
Don't go there! When someone hit a touchy subject and you wanted to let 'em know, this is what you said.
Getting Jiggy. It meant dancing and the great Will Smith popularized it.
Home Skillet/Homey/Home Slice. A term that typically meant friend.
Hoochie: A word used to describe sluts, whores, skanks, hos, tramps, hussies, floozies and hookers.
It's all good. It's ok, no worries.
My bad. My mistake.
Not! We followed a sentence with this word using it in a negative manner. e.g. "Street Sharks are better than Ninja Turtles… Not!"
Phat. Awesome, cool and in some cases – pretty hot and tempting.
TMI. Too much info.
Talk to the hand (because the face ain't listening). I don't want to hear you, I'm not listening, here's my hand – take it up with him.
Whassup? How's it going? What's going on? Etc.
Whatever! Again, Clueless & Alicia Silverstone are to thank (or blame?) for this.
Yo! Hi or hello.
You go! Encouraging phrase meaning, good for you!

46. WILL SMITH IS THE GREATEST ENTERTAINER OF OUR DECADE.

If there were a decade achievement medal for the 90s, it would *have to* be awarded to Will Smith. Music? Will Smith made it. Hit television series? Will Smith had one of those. Blockbuster films? Will Smith made plenty of 'em, developing himself into the biggest box office success in the world. When you take a closer look at Smith's body of work, it's evident that he was the man of the 90s.

IMPACT ON MUSIC: Will Smith's contributions to the rap genre are often overlooked and underrated. In 1988 he won the first ever rap Grammy and his songs that were family friendly (e.g. Parents Just Don't Understand & Summertime) made him a massive success and popular musician well into the 90s. "Getting Jiggy With It" is a phrase that wouldn't even exist had Smith not popularized it through his music. Look, he doesn't curse, he's not going to make tunes about guns, drugs or big booty models but the man tells some great stories and discusses relatable topics in a manner that's appealing to all ages, races and genders. Will is **frustratingly** underrated as a musician.

IMPACT ON TELEVISION: Say the words, "In West Philadelphia, born and raised..." and watch the reaction you get. Anybody within a 10 foot radius will recite the lyrics to *The Fresh Prince of Bel-Air* in a synchronized session. It seems like *everyone* watched that show over its six seasons (148 episodes) and it was worthy of the attention. This sitcom delivered plenty of jokes and comedy but when it was time for dramatic or sad episodes, they knew how to bring on the waterworks. Even to this day, The Fresh Prince is a beloved series that is distributed in syndication by several networks.

IMPACT ON MOVIES: Nobody is a bigger star and nobody delivers bigger summer hits than Will Smith and that all

began in the 90s. His 90s hit films include *Bad Boys, Independence Day, Men In Black, Enemy Of The State and Wild Wild West.* Those movies all made a good chunk of money and Smith's stock quickly rose to the most bankable actor in Hollywood.

After really taking a gander at his production, one realizes how valuable to the decade he was. Can you imagine the 1990s *without* Will Smith? You're talking about a **massive** difference in our entire pop culture. The bottom line is that nobody came close to impacting three different realms of entertainment like Will Smith did. Whether it was his music, sitcom or films, he created classics and is as successful as they come.

47. AIM WAS OUR SOCIAL NETWORK.

Before *Myspace*, *Facebook* and *Twitter* existed; a little thing called *America Online Instant Messenger* graced us with its presence. The messenger allowed us to have plenty of conversations and keep in constant touch with our friends – much like Facebook does in present times. The customization of screen names, profiles, icons, fonts and colors was the equivalent to the way Myspace let one get creative. Then, there were away messages that allowed us to put our wittiness on display in Twitter-like form. Really, this was somewhat of a pioneer for future social networking websites and there are plenty of noteworthy things that the avid AIM user is sure to remember:

REMEMBERING AOL INSTANT MESSENGER

- aLtErNaTiNg CaPiTaL aNd LoWeRcAsE lEtTeRs. (sadly, there are some of you who still do this. If you're well into your twenties, c'mon – it just *has to* stop.)

- People with uncreative screen names sucked. CutiePie22099 was lame. The more numbers at the end of your screen name, the less creative you actually were. (With the exception of birth years, e.g. 1988.)

- Using the sh*t out of emoticons. This was serious business when flirting or trying to get a point across, choosing the appropriate emoticon took some thought. ;)

- The song lyrics on your profile. They were either emo, wise or you simply stole 'em from what the other cool kids were putting as theirs.

- Having signature notifications for a specific person. Boyfriends, girlfriends, best friends, crushes, or the poor person you creepily stalked, were all worthy of being given a special sound/chime, notifying you when they had arrived online.

oH, tHe gOoD oL' dAyS oF AiM. tHeY WiLl bE mIsSeD.

48. SPACE JAM IS AWESOME AND MICHAEL JORDAN IS THE GREATEST OF ALL TIME.

NBA basketball players + Looney Tunes characters = GOLD! When you take the greatest cartoon character of all time (Bugs Bunny) and combine him with the greatest basketball player to ever live (Michael Jordan), you have created something historic. Seriously, anybody who doesn't like Space Jam *is not* worth knowing or interacting with. There are just too many good things (Charles Barkley, Danny DeVito and Bill Murray to name a few) in the film to have a negative opinion of it.

The movie is actually very re-watchable, allowing us to notice things we didn't necessarily pick up on as kids. For example, there's a *Pulp Fiction* reference which consists of Elmer Fudd and Yosemite Sam donning white shirts, black suits & ties, shooting out the teeth of one of the antagonist "Monstars". Or how about the shot taken at Disney when Bugs Bunny asks, "What kind of Mickey Mouse organization would call a team The Ducks?" (Likely a reference to Disney's ownership of the NHL's *Anaheim Mighty Ducks* team). Then there were the past the radar, adult jokes sprinkled in there. Oh, you don't remember? That's probably because you were far too young. On one occasion, after meeting Lola Bunny, Bugs' entire body becomes stiff and hits the court with a wood-on-wood sound effect. There's even one scene which shows a therapist asking Patrick Ewing (who lost his basketball abilities) if his "*performance*" has suffered in "*any other areas*". Ewing flashes a look of disbelief and yells, "**No!**"

All in all Space Jam does its job. Sure it lacks character development and all that other mumbo-jumbo, but it wasn't made with winning an *Academy Award* in mind. The purpose of the movie was to entertain the sh*t out of children and that's exactly what it did. We saw Jordan everywhere in the 90s. Sneaker commercials, Gatorade commercials and whatever other sponsor's commercials aired during games in which he and the *Chicago Bulls* dominated opponents. Michael was (and still is) an icon so 90s kids are rather fortunate to have had him star in a movie for our youthful selves. Can you imagine if they tried to make a sequel? Yeesh, I see issues with a lot of the current NBA players filling MJ's role[1].

[1]POTENTIAL NBA STARS FOR SPACE JAM 2:

LEBRON JAMES: If the going gets tough, LeBron would get going... To the Monstars, where it's *easier* to win.
KOBE BRYANT: He's already had enough comparisons to Jordan for one NBA career, this would simply be one more.
KEVIN DURANT: He would probably **destroy** the Monstars and lead the Tune Squad to a blowout victory - which makes for a rather boring movie.
DIRK NOWITZKI: The Tune Squad doesn't have 13 years to spare before Dirk can finally lead 'em to win the big one.
BLAKE GRIFFIN: I'm not sure special effects people can digitally animate him to jump as high as he can in real life.
KEVIN GARNETT: Garnett's potty mouth would make for an R-Rated movie.
DERRICK ROSE: (see Kevin Durant).
METTA WORLD PEACE (AKA RON ARTEST): Space Jam with Metta would probably turn into a strange Suspense or Thriller movie, which has the potential to be epically entertaining. Unfortunately, the artist formerly known as Artest is all types of unpredictable and loonier than the toons themselves, which is high risk for a children's flick.
DWIGHT HOWARD: I can't think of a single good reason *not* to cast Dwight actually. He's got great personality, skills and he'll miss enough free throws to keep the game entertaining. Hmmm, can somebody make this happen?

49. OUR SUPPLIES MADE GOING TO SCHOOL A SMIDGEN MORE FUN.

School isn't generally meant to be boatloads of fun. Unfortunately in our younger days, if something wasn't amusing or exciting we wanted no part in it. Reading (books other than *Where's Waldo*) and writing (in *cursive*, which to this day is useless) weren't our ideal candidates for fun. Luckily, some true geniuses existed and they created stuff that turned into classroom fads. These trends made getting out of bed to prepare for school just a bit more doable.

90s CLASSROOM FADS & TRENDS.

Gel Pens: They were geared towards girls but artsy and intrigued dudes couldn't pass on such a festive writing utensil! We wrote on the hands of ourselves and our peers with 'em, we used 'em on notes that we passed around and for a short period of time, they were even used on our classroom assignments. Unfortunately an inevitable backlash came along when people realized how easily smeared or obnoxiously illegible the ink was. Teachers turned into Gel/Milky Pen Nazis who only accepted blue or black ink and pencils. The downside of the pens can be seen firsthand now if you possess any old notes or yearbooks with messages from friends, you'll see that they are now a sparkly, glistening, indecipherable mess.

Trapper Keepers: Regular old binders aren't really that exciting. Sure, they are necessary to hold loose leaf paper and class work but they are so boringly constructed. Unless of course you take a binder, throw gaudy designs on it, create a Velcro tab for secure closing and call it a Trapper Keeper. Do that and you have yourself a hit – at least, you did in the nineties.

Lisa Frank Stuff: It was ridiculous how much this brightly colored paraphernalia filled the desks and backpacks of little girls across the nation during the 1990s. With colorful designs that featured cute puppies on beaches, bunnies performing ballet, unicorns, bears and seals, there were few little girls who could resist the urge to buy Lisa Frank's vibrantly decorated material (folders, pencils, stickers, toys, etc.)

Mr. Sketch Scented Markers: Holy hell, it was beyond difficult to not put these in your mouth to see if they tasted as amazing as they smelled. It was like *Skittles* for your nose and proof that black licorice is as unappealing a scent as it is a taste.

Pencil Toppers: They were basically ornaments for pencils that served no real purpose other than decoration, yet we loved them. *Troll* pencil toppers were a really popular one which is strange because they were actually rather creepy looking.

All in all, these extras just made those days in the classroom a *little bit* easier to cope with, but for many of us, that's all we needed. Can you imagine how many kids would've dropped out by 5th grade if they didn't have *Mr. Sketch Scented Markers* to look forward to? Thank you Mr. Sketch, for being the sole reason half of us stayed in school.

50. TOYS CONTRIBUTED GREATLY TO OUR CHILDHOOD.

One of the most amazingly enjoyable aspects of a childhood is **toys**. *Every* generation grows up with them and you can learn a lot about a culture based on what their youth plays with. Toymakers have a crucial job if you think about it. They are responsible for the early years of our lives, where we get to be carefree and worry about *absolutely nothing* but eating, sleeping and simply *being a kid.* We all remember a few specific toys that were our favorites and if you were a mainstream toy seeker, surely you'll recall some of the following.

NINJA TURTLES & POWER RANGERS ACTION FIGURES: These were a little boys dream and if you were really dedicated, you pursued a complete collection that include less popular characters from each series like Bebop & Rock Steady (TMNT) or Squatt and Baboo (MMPR).

TAMAGOTCHIS & GIGA PETS: Our darling handheld digital pets that we raised with the utmost love and care. These bad boys were a lot of work and I believe it prepped 90s kids for parenting in the future.

NICKELODEON GAK: It made fart noises and ruined carpets which earned it an instant loathing from our parents. Still, it had lots of activity set accessories and different versions that made it a fan favorite. Remember *Smell My Gak*? It was Gak with scents like hot dogs, pepperoni pizza, baby powder, sunscreen, flowers and pickles -- now doesn't that sound yummy for the nostrils?

BOARD GAMES: Mouse Trap, Hungry Hungry Hippos, Don't Wake Daddy, Connect Four, Operation and Trouble... Just to name a few.

SUPER SOAKER: It began with a single pump water gun that was created early in the decade but they sure as hell made some advanced innovations over the years. If you had one of the newer models you could eradicate an entire cul-de-sac when the water wars went down, *especially* if you played with kids who utilized older versions.

POGS: Our generation produced the world's most elite Pog players in existence. Back then, there were two types of people: Those whose skills were mediocre, making them hesitant to play and those who were certified assassins that would boldly challenge you to play for keeps, and often walk away with a good chunk of your collection in hand. Of course, like all great things these were widely banned in schools which contributed greatly to their demise.

EASY BAKE OVEN: They were geared towards little girls but it's safe to say that everyone around benefited from brownies & cupcakes.

CREEPY CRAWLERS: This was the boy equivalent of the Easy Bake Oven, but instead of making baked treats, it produced squishy worms, spiders and other critters.

We used all types of toys for hours upon end and that's why they are such a massive part of pop culture and life as a child in the 90s. While they may produce more hi-tech stuff nowadays, as 90s kids we should appreciate the classics that we had and revel in glory over the fact that plenty of our toys are still circulating today, with slight modifications to them. If you want a reminder of just how crucial toys were to your life, go deep into your closet, attic or garage and find your toy collections. It's like opening a time capsule and recalling all of the things that were once so important to your daily routine. I assure you it's nostalgia at its finest.

THAT'S ALL FOLKS.

(AT LEAST, FOR NOW IT IS.)

HOW 90s ARE YOU?

Read and answer each question. If you choose "yes", give yourself a point. If "no", subtract one.

1. Did you play Power Rangers as a kid?

2. Did you watch *Doug* regularly?

3. Did you spend weekend nights watching TGIF & SNICK?

4. Did you know that Uncle Phil voiced Shredder before reading it in this book?

5. Is *Batman The Animated Series* your favorite form of Batman?

6. Are Cory & Topanga your favorite fiction romance ever?

7. Did you want to be (or actually were) on a Nickelodeon game show?

8. Have you ever blown into a video game cartridge to fix it?

9. Have you ever eaten a Ninja Turtles ice cream bar with the bubble gum eyes?

10. Did you grow up watching *Rugrats*?

11. Have you ever read *Goosebumps* or Judy Blume's books?

12. Does Kel love orange soda?

13. Have you ever experienced insufficient juice via *Capri-Sun* or *Hi-C*?

14. Did you or someone you know ever wear sneakers that lit up?

15. Have you spent a minimum of 40 hours total playing Sonic or Mario video games?

16. Did you cry or feel depressed following Mufasa's death?

17. Have you ever gone hunting on Oregon Trail?

18. Did you watch *Hey Arnold!*?

19. Do you remember Bret Hart, The Undertaker and Stone Cold Steve Austin?

20. Do you prefer the X-Men & Spider-Man cartoons over their movies?

21. Did you buy either Britney Spears, Christina Aguilera or Mandy Moore's albums?

22. Did you ever order books from Scholastic catalogs?

23. Did *Are You Afraid of The Dark* ever scare you?

24. Did you ever cheat during a game of Heads up, Seven up?

25. Did you notice that Judy Winslow went missing on *Family Matters*?

26. Did you go to arcades for social gaming as a kid?

27. Have you spent lots of time searching for Waldo?

28. Was Captain Planet the first tree hugger you encountered?

29. Have you seen *Aladdin*, *Lion King* and *The Little Mermaid*?

30. Have you ever eaten Butterfinger BBs or Pixi Stix?

31. Is *Home Alone* a Christmas tradition for you?

32. Have you ever disconnected from the internet so someone could use the phone?

33. Did you ever want to ride the magic school bus with Miss Frizzle?

34. Did you ever watch *Ren & Stimpy* or *Rocko's Modern Life?*

35. Did you own ANY *Teenage Mutant Ninja Turtles* merchandise?

36. Did you want to attend *Tiny Toon Adventures'* Acme Looniversity?

37. Did you ever purchase *NSYNC, The Backstreet Boys or 98 Degrees' albums?

38. When you found out about Bob Saget's vulgar tendencies for the first time, were you shocked?

39. Have you ever caught a Pokemon? (In the card or video game)?

40. Have you sat through *Kazaam* in its entirety?

41. Have you seen The Pinky & The Brain sketches on *Animaniacs*?

42. Did you experience Disney Afternoons or Disney's One Saturday Morning?

43. Did you want high school to be like *Saved By The Bell*?

44. Did you keep up with the McGwire, Sosa homerun race?

45. Have you ever used the phrase, "all that and a bag of chips"?

46. Do you own any of Will Smith's music or movies?

47. Did you use AOL Instant Messenger?

48. Is Michael Jordan the greatest NBA player of all-time?

49. Have you ever written with Gel Pens?

50. Have you played with *Creepy Crawlers* or an *Easy Bake Oven*?

SCORING

0-10:
Unfortunately for you, you didn't experience the decade to the maximum *or* you're from a different time period.

11-20:
It's possible you're from the 90s but you may have lived under a rock.

21-30:
Perhaps you could've paid more attention and maximized your experiences a little more.

31-40:
Now we're talkin'. You're a 90s kid and you probably had very specific things that you were so passionate about, you disregarded a few other areas.

41-50:
YOU ARE A 90s KID. In every aspect of the term, you loved the decade and share that unique bond that unites ALL 90s kids. Kudos to you!

FIND THE NAME "WALDO", HIDDEN 11 TIMES ON THIS PAGE.

AWUEPALSMCHHWURELLDFHGJWIUEJSMCKDKKENR
UTOQPEUMFSLALLFLMDMJMJWMDKNKJNJNKJEHWR
UTIPSDWALDOPCMNJVJDSNDIOFSADSMAJDNKJNJFJ
NCKLRNFJNMMSNASHDGAJAJKCKPASIRKTRMSKLEIR
LFODOSJSNDKMWIRMSWMONAJRJSEKDMKMRREAIR
AITIONDMDLOSJDMNFHJKSAMWALDOMDJJKLAIDSH
NSMASJJASKJKASDKDSKSKKSKDAKSSKSDKADSKSKS
DKXMFDNJACKSNAHXEURHXAWNAPLWAWPLWJDMJ
DMSXHRITLAINHERITSKALAIFFARPLYASJMNRHTHAR
KASAKAONWALDOFVYTMAKIIWQJDSJKLSOLFMHOW
TNSJAKTOMASJSDJJSMAMAKEJFDCSITNDDJJKSAKIN
JASJDDHAJASJAMERICAJSJSDFKSKFDKDSKDHIDDEN
SAKSDSJSFJDSJDISNERYJJSIANERJDJSJSDISNEYJSJD
JSDJWALDODSJSSUBLIMINALDSJJDSJDSJSDMCNSDJ
DSJMESSAGESKCKDSKDSCKCDKSDKCKKDSKDKCVFJ
VNSIMBAMUFASAJDSJJDSDJJKTNSHORNSKSDKCMCM
ENTOURAGEMNDSDSHJJKSDTURTLEAMSKSWALDOM
SMSDMCMDRAMADJJDVSJNJERICMSDKMFMDKSMSDK
FMFSKWWFKMDSCMKJCMKCKCMTBERHJSDMCMPUN
KSDJDSJSJSISTHNWALDOHJDSJTHECDNDJNKWALDO
DDSNFUTUREDSKCKDKSMCHJBJRSKLLSJFMCMSDJNF
SSDKNSDFKNFSDNKDWALDOFSKFDSFMKKDFSNNEKK
WALDODJDSJKSFDEFIFJNTNSLWLWHJBALOOSDMSD
DSKDKSKRTUTNRAKSMFFFMDMTALESPINDNSDFMSK
DMFDMKDUCKTALESDMKDFMSKFDDSIDSJFKMDSFFH
ATEMDCKMSDJSJDMDSKDSKDKSDSKTHGFJWORKING
DFDJSDJSKDSKDFLFORMSDMSCLSDDMCSDDNMNTAR
GETJSKDLSDLDFSLLDWALDOSLCSDOFMKSMDJJSJDI
LLDDSJDSJJDSDSUMDSJSJDJSJDSINASKDFMJTNFATI
CXKMSKDSMISCMKFJJDFJFFAKEWALDOMDSMSDSSJF
KCHRITSMMDMHJJCNDCSJDJSLSMRUTOWPDSMTRIFS

DEDICATION

This book goes to my mother, Jacqueline & father Jackie, who made having such an epic 90s childhood possible.

ABOUT THE AUTHOR

CHRISTOPHER HUDSPETH is the creator of the website Things 90s Kids Realize. He has written blogs about pop culture & sports, and is currently working on anything from film scripts to novels. He currently lives in Tucson Arizona where he continues creating a variety of writing projects.

FOR MORE VISIT:

Things90sKidsRealize.com

facebook.com/things90skidsrealize

Made in the USA
Middletown, DE
28 August 2017